D1490727

# Internet Safety for Kids and Young Adults

Jeff Sechler

Copyright © 2012 Jeff Sechler

ISBN: 1481115723
ISBN-13: 978-1481115728

Printed in the United States of America

# CONTENTS

# INTRODUCTION

*What happens in cyberspace stays in cyberspace.* OK, so it doesn't have the same ring to it as the famous tag line for Las Vegas, but it still rings true. What you say and do online will remain there forever. And, it can follow you around offline as well.

The Internet is a part of our everyday lives and people rely on it heavily in order to complete work for school, find information for their jobs, apply for colleges, communicate, etc. Millions of people also use it to make purchases instead of driving to a store. While the Internet is a great place to work and play, this freedom of information is not necessarily "free." There are many not-so-recognizable costs involved.

Over the years you have heard a million different safety tips about how to protect yourself from every day dangers: always lock your doors, don't talk to strangers, look both ways before crossing the street, etc. But as our world becomes more electronic, these every day dangers turn digital and can sometimes be more detrimental if not taken seriously. There are no rules and no real warning signs telling you what to look out for in this digital world. That is, until now!

*Internet Safety for Kids and Young Adults* provides information about many of the dangers lurking online and how you can protect yourself from such risks. It is divided into three segments: Personal Safety Risks, Personal Property Risks, and Professional Risks. Each of these is different, yet they have many of the same characteristics. Each individual chapter discusses a specific topic, ranging from sexual predators to identity theft to copyright rules. The experts have weighed in on each subject and provide real-life stories about how these crimes have affected other people your age.

Sure, you are thinking these types of things only happen to other people and would never happen to you, right? Well, it can happen to you. Correction, it WILL happen to you if you are not careful with what you do and post online. Ultimately, how safe you are online comes down to one thing: YOU.

Some of the items in this book may impact you now, some may impact you in the future, but all of the threats and crimes listed in the pages of this book should be taken seriously. It doesn't matter if you are male or female, young or old. Internet crimes and injustices can happen to anyone. Everyone is fair game for becoming a victim.

Don't believe me? Ask billionaire co-founder of Microsoft Paul Allen. He had his Identity stolen in early 2012. The thief was quickly tracked down and arrested, but it goes to show that anyone can become a victim.

The Internet is called the World Wide Web for a reason—it literally connects us to people all across the world with unprecedented speed. Like a real-life super power, this ability to connect with people all across the globe comes with a great deal of personal responsibility.

We no longer live in a world of privacy. Everything about us is now available to the world in some format. The problem with this vast amount of personal information floating in cyberspace is that many people don't want the information so they can learn more about you. They want it to steal from you.

Another unfortunate reality is there are significant gaps between the Internet's dangers to kids and young adults and the level of legal, enforcement-based action dedicated to protecting you. While this book cannot do anything about the level of legal enforcement provided, it can help you by providing the knowledge you need to help keep you safe so you can avoid needing the legal help in the first place.

This information is not meant to deter you from using the Internet, though there are no apologies if it scares you or makes you think twice about what you do online. Experts agree you should use the Internet to its fullest capabilities. It provides an incredible educational and social resource unparalleled in history. Use the information provided as a roadmap for protection while traveling along the information superhighway.

# PART I:

# PERSONAL SAFETY RISKS

So, you're getting older and want your freedom. That's great! But, remember that no matter what you do in life there will always be some risk and threat of something happening to your personal well-being. Your parents did their best to teach you ways to protect yourself, but there are still things to learn. The purpose of this segment is to describe some of the ways your personal safety can be in danger while playing and working on the Internet.

# CHAPTER 1:

# CYBER-BULLYING AND CYBER-HARASSMENT

Life is rough for everyone these days. But socially, no one has it harder than kids and young adults dealing with bullies and bullying. I'm not necessarily talking about the guy at school who thinks he's tough because he wants to beat you up, though that is always a concern. Instead, I'm talking about the kid (and sometimes adult) who sits behind a computer screen writing rumors and untruths about someone as a way to humiliate or attack them.

When I was bullied in high school I simply had to worry about some guy taking my lunch money or sending me home with a black eye. I had it easy. Victims of bullying today have to worry about their picture being posted online or derogatory comments posted all over the web. With the technologically advanced world we live in, what used to be a very black and white stage of life has turned digital and, in most cases, completely anonymous. This harassment happens to people of all ages, ranging from elementary school to adulthood. Many adults,

> **Did you know?**
> One in ten children worldwide will experience Cyber-bullying.

both young and old, are victims of being threatened or harassed online just as much as teens. Bullying attacks don't just happen at school. They can happen anywhere and follow you everywhere you go. Even the safe confines of your home can be infiltrated with this hate via the Internet connection inside your computer or phone, making the ridicule and bullying available 24 / 7.

## What are Cyber-bullying / Cyber-harassment?

Cyber-bullying or Cyber-harassment are essentially the same thing, and vary only based on the ages of the parties involved. No matter what the name, it is a very serious concern for anyone who uses the Internet.

By definition, **Cyber-bullying** is when a child or teen is tormented, threatened, harassed, humiliated, embarrassed or targeted by another minor by means of Internet technologies or cell phones. It is one of the fastest growing problems facing young people both here in the United States and worldwide.

**Cyber-harassment** describes the same type of activity as cyber-bullying, only both parties are adults (over 18 years old).

For the sake of this chapter, all instances will be referred to as cyber-bullying, unless otherwise noted. The term cyber-aggressor or simply aggressor will also be used to refer to cyber-bullies or cyber-harassers. The term aggressor signifies that the person is being forceful towards someone else and is a fitting name for those who partake in this type of activity.

If you set aside the distinction between the names, you see considerable common ground between the two. Both rely on forms of digital media and both may use anonymity to engage in relentless and vicious attacks. Most cyber-bullies engage in threatening or humiliating acts toward the victim by causing emotional distress, spreading lies, or compromising their social well-being. These acts are deliberate and are done only for the self-gain and satisfaction of the perpetrator.

Cyber-bullying is rarely a one-time-and-done thing. It is typically repeated messages and communication towards or against someone. Cyber-bullies do not sugar coat harassing messages, either. You know right away if the message was meant to hurt you or not.

Cyber-bullying can occur in many different forms, some of which are detailed below. This is by no means a complete list of ways bullying can occur online, but it should serve as an example showing it can happen in just about every form.

**Instant Messaging or Text Messaging**

A person may send hateful or threatening messages to another person. It is easier to say things which are hurtful when you are not face to face with the person you are talking bad about. These messaging systems provide a virtual wall to hide behind when threatening another person.

Someone could create a screen name that is very similar to someone else's name, but missing a letter or adding an additional letter to make it unique. They would then contact other people, pretending to be the victim and say inappropriate things or do malicious activity. The other person may not realize right away that the comments are not coming from the actual friend and can cause undesirable

### Did you know?

Over 80% of teens use cell phones regularly, making it the most common medium for cyber-bullying.

results.

Cyber-bullies have been known to send death threats to victims via IM or text messages as well.

**Blogging**

Blogs are a great way to express one's thoughts and feelings. They are online diaries which allow you to write whatever you want—good or bad. Blogging provides an easy outlet for people to write hurtful or threatening comments about you or someone else. Or, they could create a blog pretending to be you, and have you come across as someone you are not and offend other people.

Many times the victims are the ones with the blog and the aggressors post hurtful comments at the end of the blog text, criticizing the person or what they wrote, often times going completely off topic. If you are not the owner of the blog, it becomes very difficult for you to remove any of the posts and information listed on these pages.

It is quite easy and usually free to set up a blog and people do it frequently to post criticisms about others and to try to destroy reputations or invade their privacy.

**Social Media**

Just like blogging, posting to social media websites is an easy way to get information out quickly. While this can be used as an advantage in many cases, it can also be devastating to a victim of cyber-bullying. An aggressor can post something on the victim's page and it is instantly seen by all of their friends (which can be several thousand). Or, maybe the bully

**Did You Know?**

Nearly 90% of teens have a Facebook account.

hacked into the victims account and then sends message or posts something as the victim for all to see.

## Creating Fake Websites

There are many free website creation tools allowing anyone with access to the Internet to create a webpage. Many times, people create pages about someone else containing compromising images or information, most of which is probably not true at all, all in an effort to humiliate or cause harm to the victim. Just like blogs, it is very difficult for a victim to have one of these websites deactivated (notice I did not say deleted) from the Internet.

## Email messages and pictures

Most schools have their own email system these days, which makes it a prime resource for harassment in a hurry. All it takes is for one person to be upset with someone else and want to cause some embarrassment or harm and they send an email to the entire directory. Sure, the aggressor may be more likely to get caught by using a school resource, but the threat of being caught doesn't necessarily stop them. And by that point, the damage has been done. They may be punished for a few days or weeks, but the pain it causes the victim can last a lifetime.

Also, with the ability to create an email address for free in a matter of minutes from any number of online resources, people every day are creating and using alias email accounts as a means to communicate with someone without the victim knowing who they really are. These messages can consist of simply words or can contain unwanted materials such as images, viruses, or videos. The presence of cameras on cell phones has enhanced the ability to take a picture quickly and send it to hundreds of recipients easier than ever.

## Sending Unwanted Sexually Explicit Materials

Bullying does not have to be verbal or written. It can come in the form of unwanted images or videos being sent to your phone or inbox from someone else. These images can come from just about anyone. Aggressors will sign up for subscriptions to online magazines and porn sites using the victim's email address. There are many websites providing access to this type of material for free (unfortunately) and can easily be sent to any unsuspecting recipient. You may not consider this bullying, but many people become very offended by this type of material.

## Stealing Passwords

People are smart these days. It is not uncommon for someone to steal a password from someone else and change the settings or lock the victim out of their social media profile. There are countless stories of a bully logging in as the victim and sending mean or incriminating messages to someone else.

> ### Did you know?
> The most common password in 2012 was "*password.*"

## Impersonation

This goes hand in hand with the stealing of passwords, but can me much worse. An aggressor can steal a password and post something on the victim's social networking page incriminating someone else, or they can create a new page altogether, disguised at the person. Maybe they log in to their email account and send a hurtful email to someone who the aggressor doesn't like. By doing this, the aggressor is impersonating the victim, causing harm to not one, but two people—the victim whose email was used, and the victim who received the hurtful note from the hacked email. The same can be true if someone enters a chat room disguised as someone else. There are numerous ways in which a person can be impersonated and each is just as dangerous as the next. There are also stories about someone creating an online personals advertisement for someone else, without permission of course. The victim then gets messages from people who think he/she is really interested in what was posted on their ad, usually resulting in unwanted attention and consequences.

The methods used are limited only by the perpetrator's imagination and access to technology. Unfortunately, most cases of cyber-bullying fly under the radar. The victims are usually too afraid to mention anything about it because they were either threatened by the aggressor or feel too embarrassed about it happening in the first place. Kids who still live at home are afraid their parents would reduce or restrict the amount of time they were allowed on the Internet or would never let them chat online again.

> **Did you know?**
> 90% of all victims will not tell their parents or a trusted adult of the abuse.

The grave result of this bullying and failure to make others aware of it is that teens and adults alike have killed themselves or someone else after being involved in such incidents. It is not surprising then to constantly hear stories in the news about a student who has committed suicide or a coworker who opens fire on his office because of being bullied or harassed.

## Who is a Cyber-aggressor?

A cyber-aggressor is anyone who engages in cyber-bullying, cyber-harassment or cyber-stalking. The Internet provides the shield for these aggressors to hide behind when writing abusive or cruel messages about someone. They use the Internet to humiliate, ridicule, and spread untrue rumors about their victims.

This anonymity removes them from the immediate feedback of the victim and they do not always "see" the initial harm they cause. Many times, the aggressor doesn't even realize what they are doing is hurtful. They see it as a simple joke or game. It is not until later that the real consequences of their actions take shape. This ability to be non-confrontational allows people to say and do things online, which they would be much less likely to say and do in person.

Cyber-aggressors do not fit into a specific profile. Gone are the days of the stereotypical perpetrator being the biggest kid on the playground picking on the little wimpy kid. The new generation of cyber-aggressors is attractive, athletic and smart. They know what they can and cannot get away with—both in school and online.

Trends have shown girls are more likely to be the online aggressors than boys are. Guys tend to lean more towards using brute strength and force when being aggressive. Girls on the other hand are more prone to flocking to the social networking sites and sending messages and comments through the online interface.

**Did you know?**

Girls are about twice as likely as boys to be both victims and perpetrators of cyber-bullying.

What a lot of people—teens and adults alike—fail to realize is once you put something online, it stays online forever and you can never take it back. Unlike a story written in a newspaper or magazine or even on the wall of a bathroom, these Internet messages last forever once they are posted. They can be forwarded, re-posted, blogged about, and listed just about anywhere, even after the original post has been deleted. Victims are often reminded of these painful online harassment acts long after the original situation is over with.

## Don't think this should be taken seriously?

### Consider this:

In October 2012, a 15-year old girl from Vancouver, Canada committed suicide after being harassed by an online acquaintance. She would often go online with friends on her webcam to talk to and meet new people. At one point, a stranger flattered her enough to flash the camera. About a year later, someone contacted her on Facebook threatening to send around the picture of her topless if she didn't do what he wanted. The stranger knew everything about her— her address, school, friends, relatives, family member names, etc. Her picture was soon forwarded to everyone.

She changed schools multiple times, but the bullying followed her through cyberspace. No matter where she went, the tormenting words and images followed her. A group of girls from her first school even tracked her down and beat her up.

The harassment got so bad that she attempted to kill herself on several occasions by cutting herself and drinking bleach. She eventually succeeded in ending her life. Another tragic ending to a story of someone being bullied.

**Or this:**

Megan was weeks away from her 14th birthday when 16-year-old "Josh" asked to become friends with her through her MySpace account. Megan begged her mom's permission to allow her to add him to her friend list, she reluctantly agreed. A few weeks into talking with "Josh", things turned ugly, he suddenly began taunting Megan, telling her she was a horrible friend, fat, a slut, and this world would be better off without her. Megan took his advice to heart, and, shortly after reading his last message, Megan hung herself in her bedroom closet.

The boy, "Josh," wasn't a boy at all. It turns out the mother of one of Megan's friends created the fictitious boy while trying to learn more about Megan and what she did and said online. This just proves once again you never know who you are really talking to online and it is not just kids versus kids in this digital world we live in. It is not only young people who bully other young people. Adults get involved too, which can lead to some very unfortunate results.

## But only middle or high school students are victims of cyber-bullying.

This is a common misconception and couldn't be farther

from the truth. While online aggression among youths tends to peak in high school—and start as young as elementary and middle school—there is increasing spillover among college students and adults. With social networking groups, uploaded drunken party pictures, and naked-ex photos, the means to torment and humiliate on campus are seemingly endless.

Websites such as Juicy Campus, an online message board which shut down in early 2009, allowed anonymous gossip by anyone and about anyone for college campuses nationwide. You could search for your school and post something about someone else, completely anonymously. It was such a heartbreaking experience for so many co-eds who read the ridicule laden remarks others had posted on the website, unbeknownst to them. The stories were mostly untrue and told of people being "easy" or "HIV Positive" or "the ugliest person ever" or even "horrible in bed." Even though this particular website is no longer around, there are many others still out there and provide the same outlet for online bullying. The insidious nature of these sites is the fact they will only become financially viable if they attract a steady stream of visitors. The more mean-spirited the comments; the more the site thrives.

Even personal blogs can be a target of online harassment. Most blogs allow for visitors to leave comments about what was written. These responses are usually valid and geared towards the actual content of the blog itself. However, there are times when these comment areas are used for malicious and hurtful messages against the blog writer. It can be a message undermining the person's writing or even personal attacks against the author.

Seth, a college student from Pennsylvania provided this personal account of online harassment:

*"I started what I thought was a pretty harmless blog. It was a place where I wrote my thoughts, some ideas, and posted some of my own photography. Somehow or another, a group of (presumably) young kids found my blog and started to ridicule it. It started just in the comments section of the blog, but then progressed to my social networking site, my work email, and even my YouTube account. The comments were never threatening but they were rude and hurt nonetheless. After several weeks of harassment, the comments eventually petered out. I guess they got bored of me.*

*"I'm not exactly sure how they got hold of my social networking site, email, etc. I assumed it was because I had my full name, a personal email address, and where I live posted on my blog. I didn't think twice about posting that stuff in case someone wanted to get in contact with me. I also didn't have enough "Privacy Settings" on my social networking site. I guess it was pretty easy to find me with my email address alone.*

*"At first, I tried reasoning and playing along with the emails and comments. I'd write back "haha" or whatever, but they just kept on coming. Then I tried reasoning with them, telling them to leave me alone, they must have better things to do with their time, etc. But the more I responded, the more they attacked. It was pretty frustrating. Eventually I just ignored them and the comments became more and more sporadic until they disappeared."*

# But you're not a student anywhere so you won't be bullied, right?

Maybe you will, maybe you won't. But remember, cyber-bullying and harassment can happen to anyone, whether you are a student or not. For example, the ex-boyfriend of a woman in Wyoming created an ad on Craigslist in her name without her knowing it.

The advertisement read: "Need a real aggressive man with no concern for women" and proceeded to request someone to fulfill the woman's "rape fantasy." It also included a request for both physical and sexual abuse and listed the address of the woman.

One week later, the 25-year-old subject of the ad was brutally assaulted after she answered the door at her home. According to police, the woman was blindfolded, gagged and tied up. She was then raped at knife point in her living room and left bound and gagged on the floor.

The article reports the man arrested and charged with the assault said he was only obliging someone he thought really wanted to be raped. The victim's ex-boyfriend was also charged after police determined he posted the ad and had follow-up correspondence encouraging the perpetrator to carry out the rape, all the while pretending to be the woman.

Police agencies have long complained about how many online classifieds ads are little more than posts for prostitution. Local law enforcement agencies continue to peruse these sites daily, easily spotting the ads which appear to be thinly-veiled promos for prostitution. It is unfortunate the "rape ad" placed in the Wyoming version of Craigslist was not caught in time to save a young woman from a vicious assault.

This particular case of harassment initiated online, but was actually enacted offline. Situations like this are not uncommon. Many times the harassment begins online and continues into the real world, and vice versa. It can completely shut down, or in extreme cases, end a person's life. These stories are just a few of many variations of the same hard to swallow truth—there are people out there who find joy in harassing and exploiting others.

> ### Did you know?
>
> Not all advertisements on Craigslist and other classifieds pages are legitimate.

## What can you do if you are being cyber-harassed / cyber-bullied?

○ **Tell someone.** Tell a trusted friend or adult and keep telling them until action is taken. There are always people who love and support you. Don't forget that!

○ **Out of sight, out of mind.** Never open, read or respond to messages from the aggressors.

○ **Tell your school.** If it is school related, tell your school. All schools have solutions in place to help you, even colleges.

○ **Keep the evidence.** Do not erase the messages. Keep them in case they are needed as evidence.

○ **Call police.** If there is a threat of physical harm, do not hesitate to call the police. A threat is a threat no matter what form it comes in and should always be taken seriously.

# How can you prevent bullying from happening to you?

To be honest, you can't. If someone wants to say something bad about you or spread rumors and untruths, they will find a way to do it. While there is no way to prevent every single person from putting things online about you, you can help yourself by remembering these few tips:

- **Keep your social networking site clean.** If someone is accusing you of something, don't have anything on your social networking site giving people reason to think you are what the bully implies. This includes pictures, bumper stickers, blogs, etc.

- **Keep your lips sealed.** If you make a mistake with relationships, sex, drugs, or anything else, don't go around broadcasting it. Sure, other people may have witnessed it, but ask them to keep their mouths shut too.

- **Let it blow over.** Sometimes you think things are a lot worse than they actually are. For a few days people may be talking about your incident but just wait until next weekend, when someone else will make bigger and more humiliating mistakes.

Ultimately, you are the cure to this type of harassment. By speaking out about something you know is happening, it will make the Internet a safer place for everyone, including yourself. Remember, no matter how much you might think people are against you, there is always someone there to love and support you and help you get through everything.

> ## Remember:
> Victims are never alone. If you are a victim of cyber-bullying, tell someone—anyone. For every bully, there are at least ten people willing to step in and give you the support and love you need to overcome the hurtful acts and carry on.

## Cyber-Stalking

Another form of online harassment not discussed as often but which is very prevalent in today's society is cyber-stalking. Cyber-stalking is a variety of behaviors involving repeated threats or harassment by the use of electronic mail or other computer-based communication that would make someone afraid or concerned for their safety.

Cyber-stalking is very common amongst teens and college aged students. In fact, the college-aged crowd is one of the most susceptible to cyber-stalking. The close proximity of the students' living situations increases the threat because most college campuses provide easy access to class schedules, phone numbers and email addresses. Cyber-stalkers can easily look up your name, phone number, office or apartment address, email address, etc. All this information is obtained simply by looking through the school's directory. Given this information, they can easily look up a profile on a social networking site or find other information about you.

Every one of us could be considered cyber-stalkers—to a degree—whether you realize it or not. Have you ever browsed the profiles in a social networking site to see what guy or girl was cutest and seemed most interesting to talk to? While these actions seem innocent enough, it is also considered cyber-stalking. Sure it is a very mild form, but cyber-stalking can also be so much worse.

**For Example:**

Amy was found by her stalker using online technology. A man was able to get her place of employment and Social Security Number by paying an online investigations agency a mere $154. They easily obtained her relevant information from a credit agency report and gave it the man. None of the people giving out Amy's personal information took responsibility to find out why he needed it. Had they known, they likely would not have provided it to him. The man wanted the information so he could track Amy down and kill her. He went to the workplace of the 20-year old woman and shot and killed her as she got into her car.

Amy's situation may be an extreme case, but it shows the power someone can have with a little bit of information. A cyber-stalker can wreak painful havoc, which is very frustrating and long-lasting. Unfortunately for the victims, the technological tools used by these cyber-stalkers are commonly found online for affordable prices, making it easier for the stalkers to continue their advances. Spyware programs are readily available and can be secretly installed on your computer or phone without you even knowing it. These programs can then send the stalker information about what you are doing when on the computer, what websites you are looking at, who you are talking to, even where you are currently located. They can also retrieve your passwords after you enter them into websites or steal your bank account and credit card information after purchasing things online. The opportunities are almost endless.

Sound scary? It should. People have become so complacent about their information and how it is stored and managed online they have no idea how easy it is to access essential personal data required to unlock the safeguards to finances, personal safety and their lives.

## What can you do to protect yourself from Cyber-stalking?

If the idea of cyber-stalking makes you feel uneasy, that's good. The discomfort you feel shows you need to be alert and aware of the Internet. Here are a few tips to help keep you from becoming a victim of cyber-stalking:

o **Never reveal your home address.** You can use your work address or rent a private mailbox. Just don't have your home address readily available online.

o **Password protect all accounts** including cell phones, land lines, e-mails, banking and credit cards with a secure password which would be difficult for anyone to guess. Change it every year. Your secret questions should not be easily answered either.

o **Be suspicious of any incoming emails, telephone calls or texts asking you for your identifying information.** The "Caller ID Spoof" can mimic someone else's caller ID or email address. It is very easy for a cyber-stalker posing as a banking representative, utility, credit card representative or your cell phone provider to obtain your personal private information. If you are suspicious hang up and call or email the institution directly to be sure you were not a target of a cyber-stalker.

o **Never give out your Social Security Number** unless you are absolutely sure of who is asking for it and why they need it. This number gives a cyber-stalker easy access to every part of your life.

o **If you are leaving a partner, spouse, boyfriend or girlfriend**—especially if they are abusive, troubled, angry or difficult—**reset every single password on all of your accounts to something they cannot guess**. This will prevent them from hacking into your accounts and causing trouble.

o **If you think you're a victim, have your PC checked by a professional**. If you are experiencing cyber-stalking incidents, your computer may already be compromised. Have someone who knows what they are doing check it for spyware and other viruses.

o **If you think you have a cyber-stalker, move fast**. Lots of people don't take action because they think they're crazy or imagining things. Record incidents—time, place, event. Victims of repeated attacks tend to become paralyzed with fear. Meanwhile, cyber-stalkers often get such a rush off the first attack it encourages them to keep going. The faster you take action and block their ability to hurt or harass you, the sooner they lose interest in their project. Also, keep any and all correspondence with the person as evidence later.

o **Never post online where you are located.** By posting where you are, you are opening the door for a stalker to come find you. Cell phones with GPS enabled has made this less relevant because a stalker could install a program on your phone which will tell them exactly where you are located.

While there is no absolute way to prevent someone from bullying or stalking you, you do have the ability to prevent some things from happening. By doing many of the things listed in this chapter, you will be protecting yourself from many of the dangers waiting for you on the Internet. A few simple precautions now can save you a lot of hassle in the future.

# CHAPTER 2:

# TEXTING AND SEXTING

Ah, cell phones and text messages. Where to begin? What happened to the days in the not too distant past when a phone was used for actually dialing a number and talking to someone? You know, those little holes on the top and bottom of the phone are not just there for decoration. They are actually used for speaking and listening to hear other people speak.

All right, all kidding aside, teens and young adults have become consumed with sending text messages to one another. It is not uncommon for someone to be texting at home, at school, in the car (whether you are driving or riding), walking somewhere, etc. Many of you probably even have your phone in your bed with you, just waiting to see who will text you next.

There are reports of people sending three, four, or even five thousand text messages in a month. You have probably even topped that number. A recent study by the Pew Research Center shows 1 in 3 teens

> **Did you know?**
> The average teen age 12-17 sends nearly 60 text messages per day.

sends more than 100 text messages a day. This is in stark

contrast to the amount of actual phone calls being made: on average 5 calls per day. The fact is, texting has replaced actual talking when it comes to communicating.

While this isn't saying texting is either good or bad, it is important to recognize even this type of communication can have its downsides. The evolution of text messaging has developed a new language of sorts. It is a language all unto itself. Most parents of kids with phones would have no idea what they are reading if they were to stumble across your conversation, which is part of the reason for its arrival. That and it is so much faster to type "btw" instead of "by the way."

## Texts are forever

Just like everything you do on a computer is recorded, the same can be said about using a cell phone. All of those text messages you send and receive are being recorded by the phone company you use, as well as by the company of the person you send it to. Have you ever actually looked at your phone bill when it arrives? Many companies will actually print out every one of the text messages sent and put it in the bill. Others will just show you the total number and how much it will cost you if you go over your limit (thank goodness for unlimited texting plans). The point is, texting is not as anonymous as you may think and is not a one-time-and-done event.

There are even websites programmed to take text messages from people and post them on their pages. One particular website posts hundreds of text messages sent the night before. Most of these texts are sent by young adults who were out partying or are in class. They reference boyfriends or professors or parties from the night before. The site is intended for entertainment purposes only and does not give the phone number from where the text was sent, so you cannot track someone through this site. However, it does serve as a source of public humility and embarrassment if your text should appear on this site, or if the text should be about you. There are other sites like this as well and proves once again that things you do in the digital world never go away.

As mentioned in Chapter 1, technology is playing an increasing role in cyber-bullying. Text messaging is fast becoming one of the major tools used by these cyber-bullies. It is easy to type up a quick text and send it to someone. Since you are not face to face, you are more likely to write something you would not say in person. The first text leads to another, and another, and another, and another, and so on. Maybe the bully gets their friends involved and send the victim hundreds or thousands of texts to overload their inbox. The possibilities are endless.

Sometimes you can block your number from showing up on the recipient's phone, thus making your text seem anonymous. Many times though, you cannot block your number which makes your text come through as plain and identifiable as a normal phone call. In any case, cell phone numbers can be easily traced back to the person who sent it. These messages, if malicious, can also be used against you as blackmail, or if the situation is more extreme, as evidence in a lawsuit, so be careful what you text.

## A whole new language

One of the major detriments of text messaging is the overall decline in spelling, grammar, word choices and writing complexity. This new acronym-driven language is depleting the skills needed to write complete sentences and paragraphs. This isn't to say you aren't able to form perfectly worded sentences, but the longer you go without using a skill, the more likely you are to forget how to use it.

How many times have you accidentally typed the "texting" version of a word instead of the correct, full-length version while writing a paper or report? Sure it sounds crazy for someone to do this, but it does happen. Educators across the country are noting a drastic change in the way students write because of the increased use of texting and instant messaging programs. They have noted a decrease in grammar and general language usage during writing assignments and other communication activities.

Next time you text, try taking a few extra seconds to write out your words instead of using the short-hand acronyms. Believe it or not, your friends will still understand what you are saying when you write "What are you doing?" instead of "wyd."

## Driving and Texting

Another major issue with text messaging on cell phones is the distraction it causes the people doing it. Not a day goes by when someone gets run into on the sidewalks because of someone else staring at their phone. Their eyes were more focused on the keypad in front of them than they were on their surroundings. This distraction is magnified significantly if you are texting while driving a car. This phenomenon has become such a major issue that many states have enacted laws making it illegal to text while driving. Anyone found guilty of writing, reading or sending a text message while driving would be fined upwards of $100. Some states set the fine even higher with the potential of points being added to your license or jail time. A few states prohibit the use of handheld cell phones altogether.

We hear stories all the time about people being involved in auto accidents because of texting. It is the longest eyes-off-the-road distraction of all activities drivers typically engage in. While looking at a

> ## Did you know?
>
> If going 55mph, in the 5 seconds you are looking at your text, you will have driven the length of an entire football field without looking at the road!

text, a person is distracted for a minimum of 5 seconds. That doesn't sound like very much time, but if you are traveling at 55mph, this equals driving the length of a football field without looking at the road! Drivers are up to 23 times more likely to be involved in an accident than if they were not texting.

It is hard enough for young drivers to pay attention to the road and learn how to handle this newly acquired freedom. The increased distraction of texting can make things even more dangerous and difficult. Search the Internet for teen driving accidents and you will find many of them will involve the use of cell phones and texting.

> ## Did you know?
>
> In 2011, at least 23% of all auto collisions involved the use of cell phones.

Don't think texting while driving is a serious issue? Neither did Mary, a college student from New York state. She was out driving one night and texted an acquaintance. She lost control of her vehicle and rolled several times, killing her instantly. Police were able to determine she sent a text message at 1:37am, but did not open a message sent to her phone at 1:38. They reasoned that Mary was texting and the distraction of sending messages was the cause for the fatal crash.

If it is so important and you feel you absolutely must reply back to a text or a phone call while you are driving, pull over before making your response. Anytime you do something distracting on the roadway, you put not only yourself in danger, but you put everyone around you in danger as well.

> ### Did you know?
> Texting while driving is more dangerous than driving under the influence of alcohol.

## "Sexting"

And then there is the creatively dubbed "sexting" phenomenon. It seems just about everywhere you turn you hear stories about teens or young adults sending naked or half naked pictures of themselves to other people. This act of sending sexually explicit pictures or messages via your mobile phone is what is referred to as sexting. Older adults do it too, so you are not alone in this regard. Maybe you've even done it. It is a very common occurrence. Recent studies have shown that nearly twenty percent of teenagers and one-third of young adults 18 to 26 say they had electronically sent or posted online nude or semi-nude pictures of themselves. They also found slightly more girls than guys said they had sexted. Most of the respondents said it was fun and flirtatious to send these messages. Nearly half of the girls who responded said they were pressured into it by a guy. Less than one-fifth of the male respondents said they were pressured into it.

You know how it works: your significant other asks you to send them a picture of you with your shirt off or in your swimsuit, or maybe something even racier. You oblige because you really like them and don't want to upset them and have them think you don't care for them. You pull out your phone and snap a quick picture and hit send, not thinking twice about doing it. Depending on your relationship, that person may send a picture back to you and the back and forth continues with several more pictures. It is easy to see how this act can be exciting.

## Sexting is not always fun and games

Sending these racy images seems innocent enough, right? You trust the person you are sending it to enough to think they would never do anything with the picture other than use it for their own viewing pleasure. Most teens and young adults are naïve enough to think this way. Unfortunately, it doesn't usually work like that. Everyone likes to show off their cute girl or boyfriend to their friends. It makes them feel good inside. It is very likely the picture you sent to your significant other will be shown to their friends, either on their own phone, or by them forwarding it. Now the original picture, which was intended for only one person to see, has spread to others. These other people have no reason not to pass it on and can send it to their friends, who then send it to their friends and so on. Pretty soon everyone in town knows about the picture. It can be pretty embarrassing depending on the type of picture it was.

Even if the original recipient was respectful at first and didn't send it out to their friends, what happens if you break up with this person? Will they delete it? Possibly, if they do not hold grudges. Or, which is more often the case, they could be angry with you and send the picture to all of their friends, who then send it to their friends, and it explodes and spreads like a plague. A seemingly innocent photo you sent to your ex is now coming back to haunt you just like that.

Think your friends are trustworthy enough to not disrespect you by forwarding your picture? So did Jessica, an 18 year old girl from Ohio. She sent nude photos of herself to her boyfriend. When they broke up, he sent them to other girls at their high school. Those girls started harassing her, calling her a slut and a whore. Jessica became miserable and depressed and even afraid to go to school. After several months of the ridicule and abuse, Jessica killed herself. She ended her life because a picture she took of herself got into the wrong hands.

Then you have the story of a 13-year old girl who hung herself after a topless picture of her circulated around her school. It is happening all the time and not just to those in small towns. It was not too long ago a high profile actress from a certain children's cable network was caught in the midst of a sexting scandal, too. It only takes one picture, one time, to get into the wrong hands and cause havoc for the victim.

There is also now another option for your image to be distributed. A website was launched in recent years allowing people to upload their "sexts" and post them for everyone to see. This works in the same way as the website which takes texts from the night before and posts them online. A person can upload an image to the website and be completely anonymous about it. The only identifier is the area code in which the sext was sent from. The site is easily accessible with a quick internet search and there are no security measures in place to prevent people from viewing these images. The site should be considered pornography and there is no guarantee the subjects are over the age of 18, so view at your own risk. Do you want to run the risk of having your image online for the world to see? They could easily end up in the hands of an online predator, which can cause an entirely different problematic situation. Once in cyberspace, these photos and any potential consequences are out of your control.

## The consequences of sexting are not just social

Along with the torment of your friends and peers, there can also be some major legal penalties involved with sending and receiving these racy images. It is illegal to take a picture of a naked or nude underage person, regardless of the age of the person taking the picture. It is also illegal to store or transfer such a picture. If you are under 18 and you photograph yourself in racy

> ### Did you know?
> Sexting is illegal in many states with fines up to $1,000 and possible jail time.

images, you can be charged with manufacturing child pornography. If you send it to someone, you can be charged with disseminating child pornography. And if you receive the image, you can be charged with possession of child pornography.

Along with these charges comes the potential of having to register as a sex offender, forever labeling you as a criminal for something as simple as taking a picture of yourself. Even at the age of 18, if it was sent to someone who is under 18, it's considered disseminating pornography to a minor. The potential is there for criminal charges. The severity of these charges varies from state to state.

Those are just the criminal charges. People who have been caught with this type of material on their phones and/or computers have lost their jobs, lost scholarships, been kicked out of school, lost friends, were looked down upon by family members and more. It only takes a few seconds to really mess up the rest of your life.

## People don't really get in trouble for this do they?

Oh yes they do. Six teenagers at a western Pennsylvania high school were arrested and charged with the manufacturing and dissemination of child pornography. The police say they charged two 14-year old girls and a 15-year old girl for sending their boyfriends (16 and 17 years old) pornographic photos. The boys were charged with possession of child pornography.

Then you have this incident. Philip, a student in Florida is now a registered sex offender because of a sexting incident. He had just turned 18 when he sent a naked photo of his 16-year old girlfriend—a photo she had taken and sent to him—to dozens of her friends and family after an argument. Police arrested Philip and charged him with sending child pornography—a felony— to which he was convicted. He was sentenced to five years of probation and required by Florida law to register as a sex offender. He is now listed on the registered sex offenders list beside people who have raped children, molested kids and worse, all because he sent out one picture of a 16-year old girl. An unfortunate consequence to a seemingly innocent action

## What can you do to prevent your picture from getting out?

There is really only one way to prevent a picture of you from getting into the wrong hands. Don't take one of yourself and don't allow anyone to take one of you to begin with. It's just like getting pregnant. If you don't have sex, you can't get pregnant. If you do have sex, there is always a chance you will get pregnant. It is a risk versus reward situation. Is the satisfaction you get by sending one of these photos to a friend or significant other worth the risk of it being put out there for everyone to see? This question is not something this book can answer for you. Just remember though, if there is no picture for people to distribute, then there is no chance of you getting ridiculed or embarrassed or having any kind of backlash from it.

If you receive a photo you consider inappropriate, do not forward it to anyone. Delete it. You can still be charged if you have the image on your computer or phone. Also, if you are underage, tell your parents. Tell them exactly how you got the image and where it came from so they know how to best handle the situation. If they know the truth, they can help you stay out of trouble.

If a friend of yours is sending these types of images, talk to them about it. Inform them of the dangers and legal consequences of their seemingly innocent actions. It can save your friend a lot of serious stress later by just letting them know what they are doing can come back to haunt and potentially ruin their lives.

# CHAPTER 3:

# INTERNET ADDICTIONS

The population of cyberspace is increasing with every passing minute, but along with this growth is the more worrying observation showing more and more people are finding it difficult to log off. The Internet, like a drug, is pulling more and more people into its never-ending supply of games, chatting, gambling and information sources. This inability to remove oneself from the web has been dubbed Internet Addiction Disorder (IAD). While this is being diagnosed as an actual problem by many professionals, there are some who still do not recognize Internet Addiction as a disorder.

Whether it is officially diagnosed or not, having an addiction to the Internet is a very serious situation. Many people are so preoccupied with using the Internet they are unable to control their use and are jeopardizing employment and relationships because of it. The concept of Internet addiction has been proposed as an explanation for this uncontrollable, damaging use of technology.

A study at a university in Maryland asked students to give up all media for one full day. This includes cell phones, instant messaging, television, radio, computers, etc. The study found that even after only 24 hours, many of the participants showed signs of withdrawal and anxiety and the inability to function without their social connections. This evidence strengthens the notion that people today are becoming increasingly more reliant on the technologies around them and have a hard time separating themselves from it.

Internet addicts don't steal to pay for their habits. They don't lock themselves in a room and shove needles in their arms or snort things to get high. Their addictions don't cause accidents or impair their judgment or ability to make decisions (usually), but that doesn't mean Internet addiction is not dangerous. Internet addictions have broken up

> ### __Did you know?__
> 1 in 8 Americans experiences signs of Internet addiction.

marriages and friendships. They've torn apart families and gotten in the way of school and work. Since it is not considered as life-threatening as a drug addiction, it is not always diagnosed, and if it is, it is typically considered more acceptable because of it doesn't pose the same dangers to other people.

The Internet attracts so many people to it because it provides us with something they don't have in real life: anonymity. People who are shy or have trouble speaking to others can easily go online and engage in intense conversations. Those who think they may be unpopular or unattractive often go online to find friends who are like them to help cope with their shortcomings. There is almost no need to even leave the house anymore. You can go online to shop, date, play games, and gamble. You can even engage in sexual activity online. It is easy to see how someone can get hooked.

# What do people get addicted to online?

People become addicted to any number of online activities. Some of the more popular things people claim to become addicted to include cybersex/cyber-pornography, having online affairs, online gambling, online gaming, and online shopping. While many of these addictions may take place on the Internet, the root of the problem is sometimes found outside of cyberspace. If you want to know about the mental or environmental issues at play, you should go see your psychologist. This book is focused on the Internet though, so the online world is where the subject will remain. Here's a little more detail about the top addiction causing online activities:

**Cybersex / Cyber-porn:** Estimates suggest one in five Internet addicts is engaged in some form of online sexual activity. This can include viewing sexually explicit images or videos or even engaging in erotic chats. It seems people who have low self-esteem or have a negative mindset about their personal appearance are more likely to develop an addiction to cybersex / cyber-porn. It is becoming increasingly more common for people who have never had a problem with sex addiction offline to become addicted to online sex. Online users can conceal their age, marital status, gender, race or appearance. They can turn to a chat room to live out a cyber-version of a sexual fantasy. Addicts use this anonymity to experiment and explore things they would never do in real life.

This type of addiction can come with a cost. You must be eighteen years old to legally be able to view this type of material. However, even if you are of legal age, if the materials you are viewing or the person you are chatting with is a minor, there could be serious criminal charges brought against you. It is not unheard of for someone to be arrested for having illegal pornographic materials on their computer or cell phone.

**Online Affairs:** Online affairs are just like affairs in the real world, only without the physical aspect of the relationship. These relationships are formed by chatting with someone through a chat room, instant messenger or even social networking and dating websites. The bonds between the two individuals become real and the communication and feelings are authentic. Many people rationalize an online affair is not really cheating because it does not involve anything physical. They believe it is harmless flirting and continue to do it. However, the emotional pain and devastation caused to a once warm relationship is still the same.

Online affairs are accounting for a growing number of divorce cases and relationship break-ups. Judges often consider online affairs to be the same as offline, real life cheating and take the side of the offended spouse or significant other. Partners who learn of an online affair feel betrayed, hurt, jealous and angry knowing someone would choose a person on the computer (who many times the accused has never met in person) over them. Often, suspicious actions by the accused throw up some warning signs hinting something might be going on. For instance, the accused suddenly demands privacy at the computer or moves it so no one else can see the screen and often ignores the relationship while spending hours in front of the computer. If you or someone you know find yourself in a situation such as this, it is important to talk to the person having this suspected online affair. Like any relationship problem, with some communication and work, these issues can usually be dealt with.

**Online Gambling:** The Internet has brought with it an influx of online casinos which have turned into a multi-billion dollar industry. While compulsive gambling has been around for decades, the easy access and opportunities available on the Internet make this an even larger problem in recent years. With the incorporation of poker tournaments and television programs where people win millions of dollars by playing cards, many young adults are taking to the Internet to learn how to play. Players sign up for a variety of websites and can play for hours on end in hopes of winning money or entry into one of the exclusive tournaments. Young adults who seek admission to an online gambling site can usually freely enter, without anyone verifying their age.

> **Did you know?**
>
> One in ten people has an online gambling addiction.

This would be a good time to mention while many of these sites are perfectly legitimate, there are always websites out there who claim to be able to grant you access to these tournaments and ask you to pay a fee to play their game, while really they cannot give you anything in return. Be sure to do some research before you pay to play. Make sure it is a reputable site – but don't get too hooked!

As with any addiction, people with addictions to online gambling tend to show an increased need to bet more money more frequently. They get caught up in the excitement of the gambling experience and anonymity of gambling from their own home or computer as they can easily hide their habit from friends and family. Online gambling has been linked to several cases of offline burglary and theft. The players will run out of money and need to find a way to support their habit, making this more like a drug addiction than some of the other online addictions.

**Online Gaming:** This is an addiction to online video games, role-playing games, or any interactive gaming environment available through the Internet. Games such as EverQuest®, World of Warcraft® and others can consume a player for hours or even days on end. Extensive chat features give these games a collaborative social aspect missing from other types of online activities and in many cases, provides more social interaction for the person addicted than many offline activities would. The competitive nature of the games can make it hard to take a break from the action. Gamers don't stop because they are afraid of letting down their teammates or someone else finding the sacred weapon or some other useful tool. The constant need to be involved in the game is what causes the addiction. Gamers who become hooked show clear signs of addiction: they get restless and irritable if they can't play and they will sacrifice other social activities just to play the game.

**Online Shopping / Online Auctions Addictions:** Due to the popularity of online sites such as eBay® and Amazon®, more and more people are showing signs of being addicted to shopping and buying things online. The term "shop-a-holic" has been around for ages and people typically relate it to a woman who loves to go shopping at the mall. Well, now the "shop-a-holic" person can go online and never get out of their pajamas to do the shopping. This can lead to an increase in impulse buying because of the many advertisements displayed on the screen at any given time or the "special deals" conjured up just for you or because you are shopping online.

Most people are able to shop in online stores without any issues or problems. However, when they turn to online auction sites, their problems and addictions become more evident. For many, winning a certain object provides a thrill and emotional rush. This isn't caused necessarily by the joy of obtaining the item itself, but more so by the experience of winning. It is this rush that keeps them bidding time and time again. For some of the more extreme cases, the addict will bid on things they don't even need just to feel the excitement of the auction and the rush of winning. People have stolen money from their friends and relatives to support a shopping / auction habit online. This type of online shopping addiction can also lead to hording of items and causes houses and garages all over the country to be filled with piles of useless items.

**Cell Phones:** This is probably the most common item people become addicted to which involves the Internet. This doesn't mean simply carrying your phone with you and using it to make phone calls. No. It means constantly using your cell phone to text, browse the Internet, watch videos, listen to music, etc. Some people might not consider overuse of a cell phone an addiction or even Internet related, but evidence shows it is both. Cell phones use the same type of technology computers use to connect wirelessly to the Internet.

As discussed in Chapter 2, cell phones are an everyday part of our lives and most young people are punching away at the keypad at all hours of the day. If there was a way for someone to text while sleeping, it would be done. This over use of cell phones can lead to a person being distracted from some other task such as driving or even walking across the street. The use of cell phones is by no means discouraged. On the contrary, the technologies available today and the opportunities they provide are incredible. However, instead of walking down the street with your eyes focused on your cell phone screen and completely ignoring the world around you, why don't you pick your head up and stop and smell the roses—one of the few things your cell phone cannot do for you.

## Internet Addictions don't hurt anyone other than the addict.

Not true. Consider this: a Nevada couple was charged with child neglect after their Internet gaming addiction kept them from caring for their two children aged 11 and 22 months. The couple claimed they spent so much time online, their kids where left to fend for themselves. The children were underweight, malnourished, dehydrated, filthy and suffered from infections. One child had cat urine in her hair. The couple was unemployed and used a $50,000 inheritance to support themselves and pay for the electronic gaming equipment. The couple pleaded guilty to two counts of child neglect which could potentially land them each a dozen years in jail.

## What are the signs of Internet Addiction?

There is a difference between simply spending a lot of time on the Internet and being addicted. Many of us are required to be online for school and work. Does this mean we are all addicted to the Internet? Not at all. For some people though it is impossible for them to logoff. Those who have a problem spend all of their free time online and might have a hard time tearing themselves away from the computer screen. Here are a few signs of Internet addiction:

o Preferring to spend time with a computer instead of family and friends.
o Lying about the amount of time you spend online.

o Hiding what you do online.
o Your family complains about the amount of time you spend online.
o Thoughts are always on the Internet—even when you are not.
o You logon as soon as a family member leaves the house.

## How can someone with an Internet Addiction get help?

There are several ways in which you can get help for an Internet addiction and vary depending on the type of addiction you have. Most treatment involves some type of therapy to help get to the root of the addiction. What does the addict do when online: Socialize? Gamble? Shop? Engage in sexual activity? If so, the treatment might not necessarily be to control Internet use but to work on socialization skills or addictions to shopping, gambling or sex. In fact, many argue the addiction isn't to the Internet itself but to the actual activity a person does while online.

Other therapy options rely on motivation. What will motivate the user to spend less time online? Since most people can't function at work, or even at home without at a computer, the key is moderation rather than abstinence. Like quitting any addiction, it takes time, patience and support.

# CHAPTER 4:

## SEXUAL AND ONLINE PREDATORS

One of the things people like so much about the Internet is the anonymity it provides. This is one of the things also making it so dangerous. You can be talking to someone who you *think* you know, but unless it is a friend or a relative, how can you really be sure?

Do you really know everyone you are "friends" with on your social networking page? Do you know everyone you chat with on your instant messenger or in the chat room? If you do, then good for you, but you are probably like most people and simply approve friends because they know someone you know or because they went to the same school as you. Maybe you did it because you thought they were cute and might want to get to know them better. Maybe you're chatting with people to make new friends who like the same type of music or sport you do.

The point is, unless you absolutely know everyone you talk to online, there remains the chance you could be speaking with someone who has something on their mind other than simply being your friend.

Studies have shown one in four teen girls in the United States reported they met a stranger off of the Internet in person. Nearly one in seven boys admitted to doing so as well. Most of these encounters with "Internet friends" turned out to be innocent and the "friend" turned out to be another teen or young adult. However, many times it is simply not the case. Many young people are dying at the hands of these "Internet friends" who turn out to be online sexual predators.

## Who is a sexual predator?

In general terms, sexual predators are people who commit sexual crimes. They don't necessarily have to be convicted of a similar crime to be considered a predator. These people are called predators because their behavior is similar to a wild beast strategically hunting down its prey.

Sexual and online predators search for victims for a variety of reasons. Some are simply looking for a good time and will try to arrange a sexual encounter. Others are more dangerous and are looking to kidnap their victims in order to cause bodily harm. Some may start out simply looking for a good time, but then panic when things don't go as planned. This can lead the predator to overreact and engage in a more severe crime such as murder to cover up the original crime they have committed. No matter what the initial intentions are, these predators are only focused on their personal needs and care nothing for the victim.

In many cases, sexual predators only go after a particular type of victim, such as children of a certain age, sex or race. Perhaps they have a thing for college co-eds. There is no way to predict who they will target as each predator has their own preference of victims. Predators typically do not randomly pick a victim, either. Instead, they choose their victims carefully to suit their personal desires. More often than not, the predator turns out to be someone who the victim already knows and has contact with on a regular basis.

Sexual and online predators do not fit into any particular profile. No longer does the stereotypical "dirty old man" classify these criminals. They can be male or female; young or old; wealthy or poor. They come from all walks of life: doctors, lawyers, teachers, students, clergy, unemployed, store clerks, etc. They live in cities and in rural communities. They come from every race and culture. Who knows, you may be living right beside one at this very moment and not even know it.

Some predators have committed this type of crime before and are looking to do it again, though many have never committed any type of crime before and are using the anonymity of the Internet to fulfill some kind of sick fantasy they have. This is what makes it so difficult to determine who is friend and who is foe while communicating online.

In general there are four different types of sexual predators. The first type consists of people who like to engage young people in chat rooms and talk about sex. In most cases, these relationships are only in the virtual world and do not graduate to meeting offline. It is for this reason this category of predators tends to be the least violent and dangerous of all of the types.

The next type are predators who start on basic websites collecting photos and pornography but then generally increase their level to more interactive sites, such as real-time chat rooms, where they can meet potential victims and try to bring their fantasies to life.

The third category of sexual predators are those who distribute pornography to others. They often partake in the creation of the pornography as well. Manufacturers, as they are called, tend to be in it for the money.

The most dangerous kind of sexual predators are the people who are willing to travel great distances to meet their prey, even if it means crossing into other countries. They will sometimes send gifts and entice their victims to draw them away from the safe confines of their home or school. This type of predator usually looks for vulnerable or lonely individuals who want attention and tend to be very persistent and skilled. They are very cunning and have the ability to form relationships with their victims within the first 2-4 chats and groom the victim into thinking the way the predator wants.

## Who is at risk?

Everyone is at risk. The use of the Internet is engrained in our everyday lives. People are on the computer for the better part of the day working, researching, playing games and socializing. It is this constant connection to the world that makes each and every one of us at risk for this type of danger.

Right now you're probably thinking to yourself you know how to be safe when you are on the Internet. This might be true. But sometimes, even the safest and most knowledgeable person can make innocent mistakes which can have irreparable results. All it takes is for you to engage in some type of risky behavior —whether you realize it to be risky or not—for an online predator to be able to contact you. These include:

### Did you know?

In 2011, 1 in 5 U.S. teenagers received an unwanted sexual solicitation via the web.

- Posting personal information online.
- Interacting with online strangers.
- Adding people you don't know to your chat list.
- Visiting X-rated sites.

Some people think it is fun to flirt online with strangers and to share and discuss sexual exploits publicly. If you use sexually inviting usernames, discuss sex online or arrange to meet someone from the Internet for sex, you put yourself in greater risk of being solicited by predators.

## How do these predators find you?

Predators can be found in just about every nook and cranny of the Internet. They disguise themselves as normal people and pretend to have an interest in the same types of things their victims would be interested in. They know all about the latest fads and music trends. They'll know about events going on in the community or some other common interest with their intended targets. It only takes a simple random message from them saying "Oh, I love that band too! Have you heard their new song?" to get you chatting.

This one simple message gets you hooked. You can chat with this person for a few minutes, a few hours or even days about innocent subjects such as the weather, sports, music, etc. and never think anything of it. The longer you talk, the more you become trusting of the person on the other side. This process is called grooming and is used by predators to earn the trust of their prey. Predators will take their time and mold a victim into believing everything they are told. It can take place in a short time or over an extended period. At first the conversations appear innocent, but over time, the predator will learn key facts about you without you even realizing the impact of what you are talking about. Have you ever thought twice about telling someone where you go to school or what town you live in?

## Consider this situation:

You're a college freshman who likes to use a social networking site to communicate with your friends and share your thoughts and photos. You have all the right security settings marked so people you don't know can't see your personal information. All they can see is your school and your picture. You log in to your account and see you have a new friend request waiting for you. You don't know the person and he doesn't have any "friends" in common with you, but he is cute so you check his profile—which is not listed as private. You see he goes to your school and nothing on his profile looks suspicious, so you decide to add him to your friends list without knowing anything about him.

A day or so later, you are on this same website and your new "friend" sends you an instant message. It is nothing exciting, simply a note saying "Thanks for adding me!" (The usage of the short-hand texting versions of words will be avoided so everyone who reads this will be able to understand what is being said.) You decide to write back and the conversation goes something like this:

**Him:** "Thanks for adding me!"
**You:** "Hi. Do I know you?"
**Him:** "No, but I saw we both go to school here and I just wanted to meet someone else who goes here. This is my first year. What about you?"
**You:** "Oh, that's cool. This is my first year here, too."
**Him:** "How do you like it so far?"
**You:** "It's going good, but my math class is harder than I thought it would be."
**Him:** "What class are you taking?"
**You:** "Math 101. I don't remember any of this stuff from high school."

**Him:** "I took that last semester. It is kind of hard. I could help you with it if you want."

Sounds innocent enough right? In this brief conversation, this person now knows exactly where you go to school and what math class you are taking, while you know nothing about him. He claims to go to the same school as you, but can you be sure? Since he is your "friend" now, he has full access to your profile information. He can see your full name, where you're from, your interests, etc. He can use this information to earn your trust—or to hunt you down.

He could easily look at your school's registrar list of courses to find out the building of your class. There would be nothing stopping him from taking this innocent brief online conversation and turning it into some kind of serious obsession.

Yes, this is a hypothetical situation and your conversations will probably not be quite like the one above, but things like this happen in real life for so many people. You can easily have the same type of situation in an online chat room. In fact, chat rooms are more common for this type of interaction to take place than in social networking sites. You may browse through a list of chat rooms, looking for one about a topic you like, or a certain age group you wish to mingle with. Predators prefer chat rooms because they are often not monitored by anyone and offer them the anonymity of hiding behind a screen name.

Most of us have an online profile through some type of chat service. This profile contains much of the same information your page on the social networking site has. Information such as your name, hometown, school, interests, etc. This is all considered public information once your profile is created and is all of the knowledge a predator would need. He could see that you like to play soccer and then introduces himself to you as a fellow soccer player and strikes up a conversation from there. These people are very skilled at what they do and are very wily when it comes to communicating with potential victims.

## Think it can't happen to you? So did this person...

Ashleigh was a 17 year old student at a college in England. By all accounts she was a typical teenager who was interested in boys and whose life was sometimes consumed by using her phone and social networking sites. While playing on her Facebook page one day she met a guy, Peter. Peter claimed to be the same age as Ashleigh and they became friends and started talking. After a few conversations they arranged to meet near her house. Peter claimed his dad would be picking her up and bringing her to their house to spend the night. Ashleigh asked her mom if she could stay at a friend's house for the night and walked out the door. She was never seen alive again.

The man picked her up and drove her to a secluded area off the roadway. She was forced to perform oral sex on him and he bound her arms and raped her. He then wrapped tape around her mouth to stop her from screaming. Her lifeless body was found the next day in a ditch along the side of the road. She died of suffocation. It turns out Peter was not 17. He was 33 years old and a registered sex offender. He was later arrested and is now serving a life sentence for the crime.

This situation is not all that uncommon. These predators know what they are doing and are very convincing in the relationships they forge. If you find yourself falling for someone online, take a step back and reevaluate the situation. Is it worth the risk to meet someone in person you only know through online conversations?

# New technologies open the door to predators

Online predators were given a new resource for their sexual advances with the launching of the website Chatroulette. The concept of the site is to connect people across the world in a video chat. The site is easy enough to use. A person logs in to their account, clicks a button and then is randomly shown the web cam of someone else in the world. Since each person has a webcam, it allows them to virtually meet these strangers—who sometimes become friends.

One of the major detriments of using this site though is the same thing making it so popular—the chance to meet new people via their webcams. You have no idea who, or what, you will see when you click the button to connect you to someone. Sometimes you get lucky and get a person who is close to your age, but often times you see an image pointed at something other than a person's face. A lot of sexual predators from all over the world are starting to use websites such as this as a way to expose themselves to other people. The only positive about this situation is you can easily skip to the next person and continue the process until you find someone you actually want to talk to. Unfortunately though, you are still "exposed" to whatever appears on the screen in front of you while choosing a partner to chat with.

# Don't use chat rooms or instant messengers? You are still at risk.

While chat rooms are a common melting pot of predators and victims, online predators also like to lure their prey through Internet classifieds sites. These are the free services where you can post an advertisement stating you are looking for a new roommate or looking to sell your car or are looking for a job. Any type of good or service you can think of is posted on these sites.

Everyone has heard the stories about people posting something online (or replying to an advertisement) for a new roommate, or someone offering a massage, only to find the person on the other end is not who they said they were. Maybe you are the one legitimately offering a service but the person who responds has ill intentions. There is no way to know exactly who is on the other side of that email address. Even after taking every precaution possible online, there is still a chance the person is reeling you in with their proverbial fishing pole.

Here is an example: a 26-year-old woman posted an advertisement on the popular website, Craigslist, offering massage services. By all accounts, this was a completely legitimate posting by the aspiring model and actress. A man replied to her advertisement and arranged a meeting at her room in a Boston, Massachusetts hotel. The 22-year-old medical student arrived at her hotel room to find a massage table waiting for him. Instead of laying down for a massage, he attempted to rob her and tried to tie her up. She struggled to fight back and he ended up shooting her in the chest, killing her. The criminal was eventually caught and charged with murder. He was also believed to be linked to another attempted robbery in the New England area which stemmed from another online posting.

This is just one of hundreds of similar incidents of victims—usually women and young people—who are taken advantage of by online predators. It is human nature to think most people are honest and trustworthy individuals who are looking for legitimate services and products. In reality though, there are an ever-growing number of predators out there who will do what they can to find an unsuspecting victim. Predators see the Internet as a fenced-in hunting ground and they can pick and choose who they are going to lure. Anyone who posts an advertisement for a product or service needs to be aware of the risks involved with potential customers.

## How do you protect yourself?

There are many ways for you to protect yourself while traversing the online universe commonly referred to as the Internet. Here is a list of several tips to follow while either chatting online or posting to an online classifieds site or updating your social networking site:

o **Pick your screen name with care.** When choosing a screen name for a chat room, social networking site, online classifieds ad, etc., make sure it does not include any identifying information. This includes your initials, birth date, name, town, school mascot, etc. Choose a unique name for each of the different discussion boards, forums, chat rooms, email lists, etc. This prevents predators from stalking and tracking you over multiple sites.

o **Keep your personal information to yourself.** Once you have been visiting a chat room or social networking site for a while, it is natural to begin to feel comfortable with the people you have been interacting with, but be very careful about giving out personal information like addresses and phone numbers.

o **Never give out your real name** – This goes along with

#2 above and is a surefire way for someone to find further information about you. It only takes a few seconds for someone to do an Internet search for your name and pull up a wealth of information about you.

o **Don't post photos online.** A predator can easily save your image and keep it. Once they gather some more information about you, they would have the ability to stalk you and know exactly who you are by the image you posted online. There is also nothing stopping them from using it in other methods and posting it on other websites.

o **Don't accept gifts from online strangers.** Predators like to lure their victims in with offers of free gifts or services. If someone offers to give you something for free, be skeptical. There is likely some alternative motive for the gift.

o **Never post where you are located online.** This applies more to away messages and status updates. These messages can work against you in one of two ways. First, it provides an easy access to a predator who wants to locate you and cause harm. Second, it provides an opportunity for someone to potentially go to your home, knowing you are not there, and rob you of your possessions. This will be covered more in Part II as well.

o **If you do meet someone from the Internet in person, do it in a PUBLIC location.** Never arrange to meet with someone for the first time at their home, your home, or a hotel room. Be sure to pick a public location so if something doesn't seem right, you have a better chance of avoiding any harm.

o **Never go to meet someone you met online alone.**
Use the buddy system. Yes, it sounds very elementary
to do this, but it is for your own safety. A predator will
be less likely to try something if he/she is
outnumbered.

o **Trust your instincts.** If something or someone sounds
too good to be true, it probably is. Predators are very
skilled at what they do and have a way of convincing
their prey they are perfectly legitimate people who
would never do anything to harm them. If you sense
something is not right, then trust your instincts. It is
better to be wrong about a good situation than to be
right about a bad one and have to live with the
consequences.

There is no surefire way to know if a person is a predator
or not. They look and act like normal people, just like you
and me. By taking a few extra precautions while you are
online, you can help prevent these people from targeting
you and your friends, family and neighbors.

## How do you report a suspected predator?

Has something like this happened to you? Are you afraid
someone could be a predator? There are a number of ways
to report a suspected online sexual predator. The easiest
way is to contact your local police department. Many police
departments have their own officers who specialize in this
type of activity and will know how to best handle the
investigation. There are also online resources such as the
Cyber Tipline: www.cybertipline.com.

If you want to locate registered sex offenders in your area you can use the website www.familywatchdog.us or do an Internet search for the Megan's Law website for where you live. This is useful to know the location of predators so you know where to potentially avoid being alone.

# PART II:

## PERSONAL PROPERTY RISKS

Along with the personal safety risks associated with using the Internet, there are also threats involving your personal property. This can include your identity, your computer, files on your computer, or even the physical property which is contained in your home. In this virtual world, privacy is relatively non-existent and people are becoming more and more savvy in the way they try to scam and manipulate the systems to access your information. This segment of the book is intended to provide some insight on some of the dangers of the Internet which pertain to your personal property. Provided are some tips and tools you can utilize to help prevent you or someone you know from becoming a victim.

# CHAPTER 5:

# IDENTITY THEFT

When you were born, your parents gave you a name. The government provided you with a 9-digit number—your social security number—identifying you as being different than everyone else in the country, or even the world. Throughout your life, you and your parents provide this information to other people, such as when you apply for a driver's license or start school or even apply for a job.

Your name and social security number represent you to people who do not know you. It is your identity. How would you feel if someone took this information and used it to take out credit cards in your name or even threatened national security or acts of terrorism, all while pretending to be you?

## What is identity theft?

No matter how it is done, stealing someone's personal identifying information is considered identity theft. This information can include your name, address, date of birth, social security number (SSN), mother's maiden name, credit card number, ATM pin number, etc. Armed with this information, someone can easily open a new credit card account, draw money from your bank accounts, purchase things in your name, apply for loans and sign up for many, many other services and programs. The unfortunate thing is, you might not even know someone has used your information until it is too late.

The Federal Trade Commission (FTC) estimates nearly 9 million Americans have their identities stolen every year and the number continues to rise. Think about what you just read for a minute. Nine million people every year—and counting. That means that every three and a half seconds someone is having their identity stolen. In the time it takes you to read this sentence, another person will have become a victim of identity theft. Chances are good someone you know has experienced some form of identity theft. It is a very serious crime. While some victims can resolve their problems quickly, others spend hundreds or thousands of dollars and days or weeks of their lives repairing the damage caused by someone else. It is not out of the question to hear stories about victims of identity theft missing out on job opportunities or being denied loans for education, houses or cars because of detrimental information found on their credit reports.

Common offline ways to steal an identity are by someone stealing your purse or wallet, standing behind you at an ATM, overhearing you give someone your SSN or name and address, or even a roommate or relative taking your information. This also happens quite frequently through phone and mail scams. And don't forget the famed "dumpster diving"—looking in dumpsters for discarded credit card applications, old cards, bank account information, etc. Those won't be discussed in this book, but it goes to show you identity theft can happen to anyone, anywhere.

One of the biggest concerns people have about using the Internet is the fear of someone stealing personal information and using it for their own good. This can be as simple as someone using your password and entering your email or as severe as obtaining your social security number and causing all kinds of financial damage.

You may think only senior citizens fall victim to scams and identity theft. Not true. While seniors are often the most common targets of offline scams, when it comes to identity theft, the younger generation is typically the best target. Why? Your credit report is usually clean and provides the perfect opportunity for thieves to cash in. Combine your clean credit report with the fact many people in your age group are sometimes naïve to the dangers of providing certain information and you can see why teens and young adults are particularly vulnerable.

According to the FTC's annual report, teens and young adults regularly account for nearly one-third of all identity theft complaints. This chapter will break down some of the most common ways someone can steal your identity and provide tips on how to protect yourself. For most of these examples, you have the power to control what information is provided to these thieves. However, there are a few instances where you have absolutely no control over what information is taken and have to trust other people to protect you against these crimes.

## Email scams:

Most cases of online identity theft come from individual scamming. The majority of this type of theft is initiated through the sending of email messages to potential victims. These messages claim they are from a certain bank or credit card company, or even from your school, asking you to confirm your information or they will deactivate your account. This process is referred to as "phishing" and is discussed further in Chapter 6.

> ## Remember:
> Legitimate companies will NEVER ask you to send personal identification information via email.

Email is considered a very unsecure way to transfer information and respectable businesses will not participate in requesting information through email. They have other, more secure, means of obtaining your information.

### How do you protect yourself?

If you come across an email you are not sure of, call or email the company who supposedly sent it to check its validity. If it is legit, then go ahead and use it, but in most cases it is a scam.

## Website Scams:

Identity theft cases done online are usually carefully planned by highly skilled individuals with very creative strategies. They create identical copies of popular, legitimate websites and try to get you to visit them by using a pop-up or an email message claiming you have won a prize. By all accounts, these sites are the exact same in design and functionality. The only difference is the fake site will ask you to submit your personal information, claiming it was somehow lost or they need you to confirm it.

### How do you protect yourself?

Like the email scams, if you are ever in doubt, instead of following a link to a website, type the web address directly into the web browser so you guarantee yourself to go to the actual page. Chapter 6 goes into more detail about online scams and how you can protect yourself against them.

## Credit Cards:

As soon as you turn eighteen, you are legally allowed to obtain a credit card in the United States. And creditors know it. Being out on your own and not having mom and dad pay for everything entices young people to enter into the buy-now, pay-later lifestyle. This is great for many people, if done correctly. I was always told it was good to have a credit card, but to only use it for small purchases I could pay off right away. This was a way to start building my credit.

This book is not to discuss how to use a credit card for purchases though, it is to discuss how to protect your identity, and in this instance, your credit card information, from getting into the wrong hands. Have you ever ordered something on the Internet? Maybe you ordered food or bought clothes or even bought music through one of the popular sites. Each time you order and pay for something online, you are required to enter your credit card information. More often than not, the website you use is secure and goes through without harm, but sometimes, if the site is unsecure—find out how to tell in Chapter 6—your information could potentially be stolen on the way to its destination. Sure, your order might still go through, but now a potential ID Thief has your information to do as he wants.

### Offline Tip:

Do not leave your credit card statements lying around. File them in a secure location or shred them completely before throwing them away. These statements contain vital account information useful for someone trying to steal your identity. This is also true for credit card pre-approvals or applications. Pre-approvals usually have your information already filled in, making it easier for a thief to sign up for a card in your name, but use it for themselves.

**How do you protect yourself?**

Be careful what sites you use to put your credit card information in. Be sure it is a secure site and it is the official site for whatever business you are using (refer back to the Website Scams). Also, pay attention to who might be around you at your computer. If you store your information on a public computer, any random person could use it to make purchases.

> **Tip:**
> Never save your information on a public computer such as in a library or computer lab.

Also, be sure to check your account balances and statements often to be sure there are no extra purchases or charges you did not make. If there are, be sure to contact the credit company immediately to resolve any issues.

## Online Banking / Payments:

Many of us also use online banking to pay our bills. This is a very convenient way to make online payments without writing a check to each and every business. These companies have made it very secure to do banking online. Online banking security is not the issue to be concerned with though. The problem with online banking and having different accounts for different websites is all of these usernames and passwords become confusing. You or someone you know most likely has all of your usernames and passwords stored somewhere on your computer. This is a very common occurrence because, like most people, you have too many different usernames and passwords for all of the different sites you use and can't remember them all. To help find the password you need, you created a simple text file or document listing them all.

Having a document like this is all well and good, but, what happens if your computer would be hacked or compromised? This information would be just as damaging to you as it would be if someone were to steal your social security number or other information. In fact, this could be even worse because they would already have full access to your bank and credit card accounts and can purchase items or transfer money to somewhere else almost immediately.

If you have such a document listing all of your usernames and passwords, make the file password protected. This doesn't always solve the problem, but it does help. Another solution would be to print it out and store it in a secure lock box or safe. This might be a bit of a nuisance to have to open the lock box every time you need your password, but it will keep your passwords safe and out of the wrong hands and protect your finances.

**Offline tip:**

Just like the credit card statements, do not leave your bank account statements lying around. Be sure to file them away safely or shred them before putting them in the garbage.

**How can you protect yourself?**

Be sure you know where you are putting your bank account information online. Also, be sure to not have a document on your computer containing all of your usernames and passwords. This is an easy way for someone to obtain your information.

## Business Computer Hacking:

Online identity theft can happen to you even if you are as safe as possible with your information. In the past few years, there have been numerous reports of computers at military bases or universities being hacked into and personal information about soldiers or students being stolen. If you were a student at a school or were stationed at a base and the hacked computer had your name and SSN on it, your identity could now be compromised at no fault of your own.

This is not an uncommon occurrence and unfortunately is one you have no control over. Thieves will target these institutions and larger corporations specifically for this information. Businesses spend millions of dollars protecting their electronic infrastructure, but sometimes these Internet hackers are one step ahead of the technology and find ways around the firewalls and encryption installed on the computers. In fact, in 2012, data containing social security numbers, names, and other information for an estimated 200,000 individuals at a Florida college were compromised. Many students, staff and even top administrators reported issues with identity theft as a result of this breach. This strongly enforces the fact that people are seriously trying to obtain this information.

### How can you protect yourself?

Unfortunately, in this situation there is not much you can do. If a security breach has occurred, these institutions are required by law to inform you of a potential compromise of your information. It would then be imperative for you to check and monitor your credit score and history to be sure everything is as it should be.

## School Identification Numbers:

Many college and universities use a student's social security number as their identification number at school. This is exactly how I was identified when I was in college. My social security number was the only way I was identified out of the 40,000-plus students at my college.

These student identification numbers are used for just about everything around a college campus, and even in many high schools. These numbers allow you to pay for items, register for classes, check-out books from the library and many other things. A lot of professors will post their grades either on a paper on their office door or online. Depending on how they do it, it is possible for everyone in the class to see everyone else's grades. The only identifier for the students would be their student ID number. In cases where their ID number is the same as their SSN number, there is nothing preventing someone from taking one or all of the other student's SSNs and using them however they want. With a little extra research, they could probably determine who belongs to what number.

In recent years, with the increase in identity theft cases at college campuses, many schools have changed their policies. They are no longer using social security numbers to identify their students. They now use randomized identification numbers as a way to help protect their students from identity theft. This has greatly reduced the number of documented cases of identity theft and has given students a better sense of safety while attending classes as these institutions.

### How can you protect yourself?

If your school uses social security numbers as student's identification numbers, talk to the school administrators about changing their policy. Also speak with your instructors specifically about how they can distribute student information without providing those numbers. It might seem like a daunting task, but with enough support, changes can be made.

## Cell Phones:

Having a cell phone as a resource for identity theft might sound a bit odd, but it really isn't. Have you ever given a friend your cell phone to use because they didn't have one? Maybe they forgot theirs at home and want to make a quick call. Have you ever forgotten your phone somewhere or lost it on the bus or taxi? It happens all the time. If it has happened to you then you know there is a small chance of you getting your phone back and no harm being done. On the other hand, the person who finds it could potentially use it to make phone calls for themselves, download things from the Internet, access your online profiles and accounts (assuming you have the login information saved on your browser), call in a threatening message to someone, etc. There is nothing stopping this person from running up your minute total or adding hundreds or thousands of dollars to your bill. If something illegal was done on your phone, it would be traced back to you, the owner of the account, not necessarily the person who did the actual illegal act.

### How can you protect yourself?

Keep your cell phone with you at all times. Look to see if

your phone has security features such as password or key lock and use them. This can prevent people from using your phone even if they find it. Cell phones often provide personal information which can be retrieved by thieves as well. Password protecting the phone will help prevent this information from being stolen. If your phone is stolen, report it to your wireless carrier immediately. They can disable the services to that phone and prevent the user from accessing any information. Many carriers now keep a "blacklist" of lost phones so that if someone tries to reactivate a stolen phone, the company has the right do deny service. Tips for how to secure your mobile device will be covered more in Chapter 8.

## Does identity theft really happen?

Indeed it does. I personally know someone who dated a guy in college who stole her social security number and other information and took out over $50,000 in loans and other cash advances in her name, all unbeknownst to her until the creditors came calling for their money. She was able to resolve the issues and cancel the loans, but the damage had already been done to her credit history. She still finds it very difficult to acquire a loan or mortgage because of the devastation caused by the ID thief. The unfortunate part is that he was never charged for the crime.

The easiest way for a thief to receive your information is by you voluntarily providing it to them without realizing it. As mentioned earlier, the most common way to have someone provide their information is through phishing scams. This will be covered more in Chapter 6, but it is important for you to know ID theft and scamming are greatly linked. Just remember, no legitimate company will request your personal information through email.

# What can you do if you are a victim of identity theft?

If you think you are a victim of identity theft, talk to your parents first. Explain to them what is going on and why you think someone is using your information. Think about how the criminals might have gotten the information. If you think you know who did the crime, be sure to tell your parents about that too. Together you can take the following steps to help counteract the thieves:

o Call one of the three major credit reporting agencies— Equifax, Experian and TransUnion. Law requires the agency you contact to contact the other two on your behalf. These agencies will place a fraud alert on your account to keep people aware of any unwanted activity.

o Dispute any bills listing charges and purchases you did not authorize. If you know of any accounts that have been tampered with, close them immediately to prevent further usage.

o File a complaint with the Federal Trade Commission (FTC). They maintain a database law enforcement agencies use to hunt down identity thieves.

o Contact your local law enforcement. If you know who might have stolen your information, you can file charges against that person and they can be charged with a crime. Depending on how the information is used, identity theft can be considered a felony with severe penalties. Also, by reporting it to police, you will have a record of the event which you may need while dealing with creditors who were victimized by the person posing as you.

### How can you prevent identity theft from happening to you?

There are many steps you can take the help protect yourself from identity theft, both online and offline. A good place to start would be to check with your bank, your doctor's office, your school or anywhere else which might have some personal information about you and ask about how they use and protect your information. Once it is in their hands, you need to trust they will do their best to protect the security of the information they store.

As far as protecting yourself from ID Theft, here are some other useful tips:

o **Social Security Number:** Never carry your Social Security card with you. Instead, keep it in a secure locked place. Also, do not share your SSN with anyone without knowing why they need it and what they will do with it.

o **Laptop computer:** Store your laptop in a secure location when not using it. Also, password-protect your laptop. In the event someone gains possession of it unlawfully, if it is password protected, they will not be able to access the files.

o **Mailing addresses:** Use your home address as the permanent mailing address instead of a temporary address while in school. This will reduce the confusion and complication of having multiple addresses.

o **Don't share your credit card:** Never let a friend or acquaintance use your credit card. They could run up large amounts of debt very quickly.

o **Photo ID:** Do not give your Photo ID (driver's license, etc.) to anyone. These could easily be copied or used in detrimental ways.

o **ATM pin numbers:** Never give anyone your pin number for your ATM card or any other credit card.

o **Shred bank statements:** Be sure to shred all documents related to credit card / bank statements containing personal information.

o **Protect usernames and passwords:** Never provide anyone with your usernames and passwords to any websites, especially those granting access to financial information.

o **Create strong passwords for your online accounts**: Make your passwords something only you would remember and would be difficult for someone else to figure out. It is recommended to make passwords at least 8 characters long and use at least 3 of the following: capital letters, lowercase letters, numbers, and special characters.

o **Check your credit:** Review your credit report on a regular basis. You are allowed, by law, to receive one free report every year. Take advantage of this and stay proactive to help protect yourself from identity theft.

o **Secure your wireless network:** If you have a wireless router for your Internet connection, secure it with a password. This free connection to your computer is an invitation for all hackers to come to your computer. If you secure it with a password, it is unlikely to be hacked into and your files will be safer.

○ **Delete old files:** If you are going to be disposing of a computer, be sure to delete and destroy all of the old files stored on the hard drive. A good idea is to run a "wipe" program designed to overwrite all data on a hard drive. Experts recommend a free product called DBAN which will completely erase a computer's memory. Be careful though, this will erase *everything*, including the operating system and all files.

○ **Install protective programs:** Install programs created to help protect your computer from invasive hackers. Things such as firewalls, anti-virus and anti-spyware programs are great tools when combating online criminals. More on this subject in Chapter 7.

There is no magic spell which will protect you from identity theft and no one is 100% safe. You should use the tips outlined in this chapter as a guide when making purchases and doing business online. Protect your information as much as possible. In this age of technology, privacy is at a premium and it is becoming harder and harder to protect the thing which matters most: your identity.

# CHAPTER 6:

## ONLINE SCAMS

> Looking for a job? We can match you with the perfect job. Just send us $100 to do the leg-work and you'll be earning top dollar in no time.

Have you ever seen one of these advertisements? If you browse the Internet, you probably have. Scams like this are infiltrating web browsers across the globe, trying to con innocent victims into sending money for a service which does not exist. If you are like most people, you feel you will never fall for a scam. This is exactly the frame of mind con artists and thieves are looking for. Individuals who think they know better than to fall for one of these tricks are less likely to raise their defenses when a criminal is nearby.

Some of these scams are so outrageous they almost make you laugh. Others are well conceived and really make you wonder if they are legit or not. You hear these fantastic stories about the "hit man" scam emails—the ones where recipients get an email to "send me all your money or I'll kill you." Outrageous stories like these help convince many people to let their guard down even more, which increases the market for scammers. The more popular ones recently are from scammers claiming to be employment agents and ask for your information so that they can find you a job. I regularly receive emails claiming my email provider is going to close my account if I do not provide them with my information.

Computer professionals hear stories all the time about how "I should have known better, but..." Every one of these people admitted to thinking something wasn't quite right with the email or link they were clicking on, but the temptation was too great.

The following is a list of some of the most common online scams of the past few years. Many of these are still being carried out, while some have fizzled into the past. No matter what though, they will serve as a good example of the types of threats lurking out there to consumers of all ages.

### Work-at-home Scams

Work-at-home scams have been around for several years, however only recently have the scammers increased their risks and amount of technology they put into their efforts. Scammers are now buying pop-up advertisements on websites and labeling them with legitimate sounding names of newspapers or magazines. The only problem is, these newspapers or magazines don't really exist. These ads have "testimonials" from people who allegedly make $5,000 to $9,000 a week by posting links on websites such as Google or Craigslist.

A victim clicks on the link, thinking they will learn all about how to make easy money through their program and are then prompted to provide credit card information so they can be directly credited for the money they earn. Instead of making money though, the scammers are raking in the dough because they charge these credit cards $60 or more and automatically enroll their victims in programs they don't want, all because the victim did not read the fine print or "terms and conditions" of the scammers hidden on other pages in their websites. The victims are then forced to fight with the credit companies to remove the charge and often do not realize they were even charged until the second or third month of bills.

Any time you hear about making easy money through Google, it is most likely a scam. It is true you can make a lot of money by using search engines, however, people cannot make money from Google by posting ads for them. Instead, you make money from Google by using their built-in advertising programs. The claim of making large amounts of money by posting links is simply untrue, no matter what the search engine.

### Job Hunter Scams

Just like the example at the beginning of this chapter, job hunter scams are on the rise with the recent events in the economy. Millions of people are looking for work and unfortunately, that means millions of people are potential victims of this scam.

It can work in several different ways. The most common is an advertisement placed online that claims the business can help a person find a job and will match you with the right employer based on your experience. All they need is $100 or so to process your claim and do the search. The

> ### Security Tip:
> Be wary when money is required up front for instructions or services.

problem is, this "business" is nothing more than a scam artist trying to make a quick dollar.

There are many honest employment agencies out there, so if you are considering using one of these places, do your homework and make sure it is legitimate before giving them any money and/or personal information.

## Email Scams / Phishing

*Congratulations! You just won the jackpot in a lottery in Africa! To claim your prize you must first send us $5,000 in processing fees and taxes. We will then send you a check for the remaining monies.*

Sound familiar? If you have an email address it probably does. Email scams are nothing new, nor are they going away any time soon. Scammers will send you an email claiming you won a prize, but in order to claim it you must first send them a certain amount of money. Some are very outrageous and are easily spotted as a scam. Others are more cleverly written and more official looking.

Scammers are very creative in the way they deliver their scams to potential victims. Have you ever received an email stating it was from your bank or credit card company and says you need to provide your account information or they will close your accounts? This is called phishing and is one of the more popular methods used by criminals. These emails are designed to look and sound exactly like it would if it actually came from the official company. When you click on the link in the email, you are taken to an official looking website.

So how do you know if it is or is not legitimate? The best thing you should do is check to make sure the link in the email is going to take you to a legitimate website. When you hover your mouse over the link, the destination link—where the link actually takes you—appears in the bottom left corner of your web browser. Pay close attention to this link.

Is it the same as where the text for the link says you will go? Does it have a lot of random letters in it? Does it look familiar but have a weird extension on it (not a .com, .net, .org, etc.)? If it looks suspicious, do not click the link.

This is how they get most of their unsuspecting victims. Many people do not realize you can determine where a link is going to take you without actually clicking on the link itself. This can save you a lot of trouble in the long run. If the link or email is from a company you do conduct business with, type in the company's website directly into the web browser instead of using a link. As noted in chapter 5, any legitimate company will not ask for your account information through email. They have better and more secure means of obtaining this information.

> **Security Tip:**
>
> Check the link to be sure it is going where it says it will.

### Disaster Relief Scams

Anytime there is a disaster in the world, be it natural or caused by man, people will swarm to provide assistance to the affected area. The natural generosity of so many people also breeds greed from so many others. Organizations set up accounts and request for you to send money to help support a town ravaged by a hurricane or flood or a community destroyed by tornados or even a college town struck with some kind of school violence. These "charities" create websites and describe how your money will be distributed if you support their cause.

There are thousands of well-respected, legitimate charities out there that really do provide your donations to the people they work with. However, there are nearly just as many fake charities only interested in taking your money with no intention of passing it on to those in need. So how can you tell the difference? You can start by checking the charity soliciting money on the National Charity Reports Index. This index checks charities against its 20 "Standards for Charitable Accountability." This does not, however, check all local charities or charities that develop quickly in response to a disaster.

You can also go to Guidestar online and do a free search for the charity. Guidestar lists over 700,000 non-profit organizations and provides information about them. If the charity is on the list, there is a good chance it is legitimate. For a list of local charities, check with your local Better Business Bureau. They typically can provide a list of charities and any good or bad information about them. When looking at charities, check to see if they can tell you specifically where your donation will go.

This type of scam is also venturing into the social networking scene. After Hurricane Sandy hit the northeast United States in fall 2012, scammers took to Facebook to solicit money and donations from unsuspecting individuals. Many of these donation requests looked very legitimate and legal, but it was just a disguise. Many respectable organizations also make use of these social networking sites to solicit donations. If you follow the few tips above, you can be sure your money is going where you want it to go and not into some criminal's pocket.

### Online Dating Scams

Have you ever tried one of those online dating services? You know the ones. You post a profile on a website describing your "perfect mate" and then other people browse the site and find your profile and you start communicating. Well, finding love on the information superhighway requires dodging some potholes and speed bumps. Con artists know by forming relationships, you are more likely to trust a person and help them in times of need. This is no different than the grooming aspect online predators use. In this case, though, the predators aren't stalking you through these dating services, though it does happen quite frequently. Instead, criminals will forge relationships through these dating web sites and after a while, convince their "significant other" to send them money for an emergency.

The scammers know how to play the love game. They send sweet poems and love letters, flowers, candy, etc. Like most Internet criminals, they can be male, female, any age, race, etc. It is not uncommon for a male victim who thinks he is talking to a beautiful woman his age to really be communicating with another man or even a 13 year old child. The pictures these scammers use in their profiles are typically stolen from the Internet, pulling yet another victim into this crime.

Even when scammers get caught by their victims, they admit the crime, but throw in the twist where they swear they really are in love with the victim. Most people will still walk away at this point, though many believe what they are being told. This is when the victims get sucked even deeper into the scam and it becomes more and more dangerous.

### How do you know if your "true love" is a scammer?

Here are a few things to consider during the initial conversations:

- o Did they immediately want to get off the dating service website and onto an instant messenger service?
- o Did their profile "disappear" as soon as the conversation

started?
- Do they claim it is destiny or fate you two met?
- Did they immediately ask for your picture or send you a picture of them?
- Did they claim they are from the U. S. but traveling overseas?
- Did they want your address right away so they can send you flowers, gifts or candy?
- Did they claim they love you within the first 24 hours?
- Did they immediately start using pet names such as babe, hun, or sweetie?
- Did they claim God brought you to them?

**Some other ways to know if it is a scammer:**

- Their spelling is horrible.
- Their grammar is not consistent with their nationality.
- They over-use emoticons.
- They often avoid personal questions about themselves.

There are many other ways to determine if a person might be a scammer, but these are a good start. Unlike normal online predators who are interested only in sex or physical contact, these scammers are interested in the financial gains obtained by forming trusting relationships.

Thousands of couples have met and formed honest, loving, legitimate relationships through legitimate online dating services. They do work, however, as with anything else done online, caution is the best approach. If the person you meet online is truly legitimate, they will understand your restraint in providing too much personal information too soon. Also, a little research never hurts—search engines can be very useful for finding information, both good and bad, about potential dates.

### Fake Anti-virus Software

You are working on your computer and browsing the Internet when suddenly a pop-up window appears claiming your computer is infected with a virus. The pop-up then says you should click on the link provided to begin your anti-virus program. Crap! Instead of running your anti-virus program, the link takes you to a website and automatically downloads a real virus to your computer. The website then states in order to remove the virus, you must pay $20 or $30 (or more) a month for their removal tool.

These pop-ups look legitimate too. The scammers design them to look exactly like professional anti-virus utilities. This is what makes it so difficult to spot the real ones from the fake ones. If you are ever not sure if the pop-up is legitimate and your computer

## Security Tip:

Be sure to have an anti-virus program installed on your computer and update it regularly.

really is infected, do not click on the link provided. Instead, close the pop-up and run your regular anti-virus program. If there really is a virus, your program will find it. Don't have an anti-virus program on your computer? Get one! You can either buy software from any major electronics retailer or you can download free versions such as AVG or Windows Defender. The small investment now can save you hundreds or thousands of dollars later.

### Craigslist / Online Classifieds Scams:

It is safe to say at some point in your life you have browsed through the classifieds section of a website.

Perhaps you were looking for a part-time job or looking to buy a new video game or even a car. There are a multitude of websites out there which allow people to post their products online in hopes of selling them. Some sites, such as eBay and other auction websites, are pretty secure because they are less likely to have fraudulent items listed, though it does happen. Unfortunately, many sites do not have these security measures in place and will allow pretty much anyone to sign up for an account and list a service, item, job or whatever else they want to put on there.

This freedom to post whatever you want is great if you have a legitimate product or service and want some free advertising for it. However, there are just as many people out there who are posting fake items and services, simply to get your information or to annoy you. If you are the one selling or doing the advertising, you have most likely received many emails about your product or service, many of which are from people who do not exist and who have no real interest in your product. The latter happens quite frequently.

I recently sold a hand-built porch swing to a nice couple in my area through the popular classifieds website, Craigslist. I posted my ad and information about the swing, someone contacted me and the deal was made. However, in the course of finding the actual buyer, I received several emails from people who also claimed to be interested, but were really scammers, trying to get my email address or other information from me. How did I know they were not legitimately interested in my product? The first tip off was their name did not look like a normal name or like a name of anyone in my area. Second, their email address did not match their name or have any real resemblance of a real person's email address. Yes, it was real in the sense it was listed through Hotmail or Gmail or Yahoo, but anyone can get a free email address through those sites. These email addresses had a lot of random letters and numbers and just didn't seem right. Another way I knew they were scammers was they did not have very good grammar or writing skills and did not really read the posting—replying with questions that had nothing to do with my product.

No matter if you are buying or selling something online, be careful who you communicate with. Never post or provide your phone number or address online. It is also recommended to create a new email address, using one of the free services listed above, for you to use solely for this type of activity. By doing this, even if you do accidentally communicate with a scammer, they do not have access to any of your other personal emails or information.

### Posting where you are

This isn't really a scam, per say, however it can have the same types of consequences. It is more of the victim giving an open invitation to a thief to come rob them. Have you ever posted something online stating you were going to the gym at a certain time or maybe listing all of your activities for the day? Of course you have. But, have you ever thought about what this simple message could be portraying? Sure, it tells people where you are going to be at a certain time. But, it also tells people where you *won't* be: Home.

By leaving an away message on your instant messenger or posting a status message on your social networking site stating you will be "in class all day" or "working 'til 8, then partying all night" you are also telling the world you will not be home to watch over your possessions. These messages can work against you by allowing predators to easily locate you and cause harm to you. Aside from the potential of physical harm, by posting where you are (or where you aren't), other types of criminals now know there is no one at your residence to prevent them from breaking in and stealing your belongings.

The scary part of this is learning someone does not need to be on your chat buddy list or even a friend of yours on a social networking site to see your status or away message. There are websites and programs available which will retrieve these messages and send them to potential criminals. It works just like an RSS (Really Simple Syndication) feed from a news network and such. Once you post a status update or an away message, your message gets fed into a system and is then distributed to the users of these programs, giving them instant access to your status.

To help protect yourself from this type of criminal activity, be sure to be vague in your descriptions on where you are and when you will be back. If you want someone to know exactly where you will be and when, contact them directly. It is not worth the risk of having something happen simply to save a few seconds.

## How can you protect yourself from online scams?

There are several things you can do to protect yourself from becoming a victim of online scams. One of the most effective is simple common sense. If it sounds too good to be true, it probably is. Here are a few other reliable tips to help you against these online con artists:

○ **Don't spend money to make money** – If an email or advertisement asks you to send money in order to receive money. Don't do it. Also, if they claim they will send you a check but you need to wire them money in return, it is a sure sign of a scam. Their check will bounce and you will be out the money you sent them with no way to track where it went. Wiring services such as Western Union cannot trace where the money goes, so it is impossible to track down the recipient.

o **Look for the "Lock"** – Any website utilizing secure encryption and allows for the safe transfer of information will have a "secure" icon somewhere in the browser. In the newest version of Internet Explorer, a closed lock icon will appear on the right hand side of the address bar in the browser. In Firefox, it appears as a button on the left hand side of the address bar. In most older browsers, this will appear as a closed lock icon at the bottom of the browser window. These icons are not just images though. You can click on it to view the site's security information. Some fraudulent websites are built with a bar at the bottom of the web page to imitate the lock icon of your browser. Be sure to check this icon's functionality before proceeding.

o **Check the address** – Another way to confirm a website is secure is to check the website URL (web page address) itself. Normally, web pages begin with the letters "http". However,

> ### Security Tip:
> Secure websites will usually start with https:// (with an s) instead of the standard http://

when a website is hosted through a secure connection, the address displayed should begin with "https"—note the "s" at the end. By checking these few things, you can guarantee yourself you are dealing with a legitimate website. It would be very difficult for a scammer to reproduce all of these items.

- **Don't talk to strangers** – Just like when you were little and your parents told you not to talk to strangers, the same can be said now in this virtual world. Sure the Internet is a great place to make new friends, but be careful. Unlike kindergarten where you could see who you were befriending, you have no idea who you are really chatting with online.

- **Do not open files sent from strangers** – These files could contain viruses or unsolicited pornographic materials.

- **Never post where you are located online** – This applies more to away messages and status updates. These messages can work against you in one of two ways. First, it provides an easy access to a predator who wants to locate you and cause harm. Second, it provides an opportunity for someone to potentially go to your home, knowing you are not there, and rob you of your possessions.

- **If it looks too good to be true, it probably is** – Use your best judgment. If an offer sounds too good to be true, then it most likely is and there is some kind of catch to it. Research the offer to see if it is really legitimate. You'll find most times it is a scam.

Online Scams are nothing new and they are not going to go anywhere anytime soon. The scams listed in this chapter are by no means a complete list. New and more complex scams are being introduced to society every day. The more you know about how to protect yourself and your belongings, the better off you will be. Be vigilant in your navigation of the world-wide-web and be skeptical of too-good-to-be-true offers coming your way. It never hurts to take a few extra minutes and research who you are communicating with or the so-called "company" requesting your information. As mentioned several times before, legitimate companies—this includes schools—will never request your personal information through your email or pop up message.

The only way to completely avoid having a scammer contact you is to go hide under a rock and avoid the Internet altogether. Since going into hiding is really not something you will be doing, by using some common sense and thinking about the items discussed in this chapter, you will be able to protect yourself and not fall victim to one of the scams.

# CHAPTER 7:

# VIRUSES AND SPYWARE

It seems like every day there is something on the news or in the papers about a new computer virus coming to wreak havoc on everyone's computers if you aren't careful. Many people take these threats seriously and take care of their machines. Others have heard these stories so many times they feel the reporters are crying "wolf" and simply don't believe the hype.

Your computer is just like a person in many ways. It can learn new things and communicate with other machines, but it can also catch a cold—a virus—and get sick. The virus can make it slow down for a while and take longer to do things or it can make it stop working altogether. Like viruses affecting people, computer viruses are typically highly contagious and can spread easily to just about any electronic device which comes in contact with your computer.

When people get sick, they cough and sneeze and send the virus into the air and spread it to other people. It is different with computers. Computers don't cough and sneeze or breathe on other computers to spread their disease. Instead, the viruses are spread through emails or documents or just about any type of program imaginable. They latch themselves onto files and when the infected file is sent to someone else, it then spreads to that person's computer and continues the cycle.

The amount of damage a computer virus causes to your system depends on a number of things, the main one being how sophisticated the virus is. Some viruses have the ability to delete files or change the content within them. Some will even completely erase and reformat your hard drive, rendering it useless. These malicious programs have also been known to scan your computer for confidential information such as credit card numbers, usernames, passwords, etc. and email it to the maker of the virus. Many viruses can install monitoring software on your computer which will allow another person to enter into your computer without you knowing it to steal information. And still others, as mentioned already, simply slow down your computer and are more of a nuisance than a threat.

## What is a computer virus?

Simply put, a computer virus is a piece of malicious software designed by someone to cause havoc on a computer. It is common for people to use the term "virus" when they are really referring to some other kind of malicious software. Therefore, it is imperative when talking about viruses to also talk about all of the other types of malicious programs infecting computers. You might have heard of things such as worms, Trojan horses and spyware being able to infect your computer. Each of these has its own unique characteristics and personality, yet each should be removed from your computer if at all possible.

Not sure what all of these are? Have no fear. The next few pages will provide a brief outline of them to give a glimpse of what they are and what they can do to your computer (and others).

**Viruses** – A computer virus is a piece of executable computer code that attaches itself to a computer program. When the infected program is executed, the virus installs itself into the computer's memory. They then attach themselves to just about any type of executable file (documents are most common) and repeats the spreading each time one of the infected files is executed. Viruses are set off by some kind of trigger. This can be a certain date or the number of times the virus has spread. If the virus is done through email, it can find your address book and automatically send copies of an infected file to everyone listed, which then infects the new person's computer and the process repeats itself. As mentioned already, viruses can cause harm to your computer by deleting files or simply slowing it down.

> ### Did you know?
> Internet Security company Symantec blocked over 5.5 billion malware attacks in 2011.

**Worms** – A computer worm is very similar to a virus. It is a program with the ability to reproduce, execute independently and travel from one computer to another. The key difference though is a worm does not need any help to travel from one place to another. Viruses need to be attached to a file and sent from user to user. Worms are stand-alone entities and have the ability to simply use the computer's network connection to spread to the next victim.

**Trojan Horses** – Named after the wooden horse the Greeks used to attack Troy, a Trojan horse is a program designed to look like an innocent, useful program, but instead is malicious software intended to compromise the security of your computer and cause a lot of damage. The difference between Trojan horses and viruses is Trojan horses cannot replicate themselves and they do not spread on their own. They can only be transmitted intentionally by email or downloaded directly from the Internet. Most times when a Trojan horse has been executed on your computer, there is a loss of data and unwanted system problems.

**Spyware** – Spyware is a type of software typically installed on your computer without you knowing it. It secretly transmits information about your online activity and the data stored on your computer. This is very similar to having someone look over your shoulder and watch everything you do online. Spyware is often installed as a component of free-ware programs such as peer-to-peer (P2P) applications (Napster, Limewire, etc.). Many times, this spyware software is used for advertising purposes, but it can also be used by criminals who want to steal your personal information.

## How does your computer become infected with a virus?

Malicious software can infiltrate your computer in many different ways. As mentioned, one of the most common ways a computer is infected is through emails. Viruses like to attach themselves to email files or even spread themselves by using your email client's address book. Someone in your address book then receives an email from you—which is really the virus—and because they know who sent it, they open the email and then spread the virus to their computer, which starts the process all over again. It is a vicious cycle.

Another common way for viruses and spyware to be installed on your computer is through the use of file-sharing websites and peer-to-peer networking programs. There are many programs allowing you the opportunity to illegally download music, videos, images, and other programs free of charge. While many of these songs and programs are legitimate (though still illegal), many of them contain viruses and other malicious software secretly attached to the files. Be very cautious if the file you are downloading is a .zip file. These are very common hiding places for viruses. Once you extract the files, the virus automatically installs itself on your computer, which can cause a great deal of trouble.

With the increased usage of social networking sites comes the unavoidable appearance of viruses into the online profile realm as well. You have probably received a message from one of your "friends" on a social networking site claiming they just found a great video and they want you to view it. Since it is from someone you know, you click on the video and your web browser asks you to download the latest version of Flash player (or some other media player) in order to view the video. Therein lies the virus, disguised as the "flash_player.exe" file. Unbeknownst to you, you download what you think to be the upgrade and instead install the virus to your computer. It can be easy to fall for this type of scam because the pages and file names look completely legitimate.

At this point, it would be good to point out a common misconception about computer viruses. Many people believe if you use a Macintosh computer (Mac) you are not going to have to worry about viruses. While this has been true in the past, it is no longer a guarantee. The reason Macs have been so immune to computer viruses is simply because they held such a small share of the computer market hackers simply did not waste the time to write them. But, as more and more people are turning to Macs (and iPods and iPads) for their computing needs, experts are starting to see more malicious software being written and tested to attack Macs as well as PCs. It is still a rare occurrence, but it is just a matter of time before Macs become a larger target as well.

## Malicious software can come from anywhere.

Malicious software can be attached to just about anything. For example, Matt, a resident in New York City, recently received an email containing a link to what he thought was a YouTube video. The email was from someone he knew and it looked legitimate. When he clicked on the link, it took him to a page exactly like YouTube but was really a completely different site. By the time he realized it was not the right site, it was too late. His computer was already infected with the virus and his anti-virus program was not able to quarantine or remove it. The virus also found his Facebook address book and sent the same email to his friends, starting the process over again. Fortunately, he was able to post a message on his page telling his friends not to open the link and his friends were able to avoid the virus.

## How can you prevent a virus or spyware from infecting your computer?

Preventing your computer from being infected with a virus or worm or spyware is quite simple if you follow a few easy steps. Remember your mother telling you to always wash your hands and to pay attention to your surroundings so you don't get sick? The same advice can hold true for your computer too. You need to be vigilant, use the appropriate tools to protect your computer and avoid contact with unknown programs. Here are some useful tips and recommendations for safe computing:

o **Update your operating system to be sure it has the latest patches** – The people who write viruses and worms like to exploit holes and bugs in operating systems and other software. Software manufacturers often send updates to fix such holes and it is important to keep your system up to date.

o **Install a firewall on your machine** – This is probably the most important thing you can do to protect your computer. A firewall is a program designed to filter information coming through the Internet into your computer. It helps to screen out hackers, viruses and worms trying to reach your computer. There are several free versions of firewalls you can download and install on your computer. A highly recommended option would be ZoneAlarm. Many experts in the industry trust this program on their own computers.

o **Install an antivirus program** – This is just as important as installing a firewall program. Anti-virus programs perform two general functions: they scan for and quarantine or remove viruses found in files or on disks and they monitor the operation of your computer for virus-like activity. There are many free programs out there, such as AVG, which work well.

o **Keep your anti-virus program updated** – After you have the anti-virus program installed on your computer, be sure to update it regularly. New viruses come out every day and if your anti-virus software is not aware of the new threat, it might not be able to detect it and your computer could become infected.

o **Run your Anti-virus software often** – You have it installed and updated, now run it! By executing your anti-virus software, you are scanning your computer for any type of malicious virus known to the program. If it finds something, it will automatically quarantine and remove it if possible. Experts recommend for you to do this at least once a week. Most anti-virus programs can be scheduled to run automatically at a specific date and time.

o **Be careful with attachments** – If you don't know who the email attachment is from, don't open it. Quite often, viruses and spyware and worms are sent through email files. Many email clients will automatically scan attachments for any type of malicious code or software, but even if it comes through clean, it could be infected.

o **Back up your files** – Just in case something does infect your computer, it is a good idea to back up all of your data and files. That way, if your computer were to become infected, you will still have all of your work and will reduce the amount of lost data.

o **Obtain your software from a reputable source** – Basically, this means you do not want to download a program or file simply because it is cheap or free. Many times these programs are loaded with viruses and programs intended to make your computer go crazy.

o **Download and install an anti-spyware program** – Anti-spyware programs work similar to anti-virus programs because they scan your system for any type of spyware programs and will remove the files. There are several free programs available for this purpose, of which SpyBot Search & Destroy is most commonly used.

o **Turn off your computer** – Whenever you are going to be

away from your computer for an extended period of time (a few hours or more), turn it off. A computer which is not powered up cannot be seen on any Internet network. It disappears. If you cannot be seen, your computer cannot be hacked into, preventing any kind of malicious attack on your files.

The first line of defense against viruses and other malware is you, the user. In most cases, you have the most control over whatever gets through to your computer. You make the decision to open or not open a file in an email or even to open the email itself. You make the decision to download or not download an illegal song from the file-sharing site. You make the decision to click on the link or not. It is all about decisions. If you don't know where the email came from, don't open it. If you aren't paying for the song you are downloading, don't get it. If you aren't sure about the link in front of you, don't click it.

Just because you do all of these things and take all of these precautions doesn't mean your computer cannot get infected. It still can. Some viruses and malware can sneak in through other programs without you knowing it. However, by taking a few extra steps and being proactive in what you do online, you can protect your computer (and your personal data) from being corrupted or stolen by an outside source.

## How do you know if your computer has been infected?

If you are running an anti-virus program, you will be notified as soon as the program detects any malicious software on your computer. Additionally, you will most likely notice pretty quickly if your computer has been infected because of how the system operates. Changes to the speed of the system or how things work are a big tip off of something being wrong. Here are a few ways to determine if you have a virus or some other malicious software on your computer:

o  Your computer starts displaying strange messages or pop-ups, even when you are not online.

o  Your computer takes longer to start or operates much slower than normal.

o  Your computer suddenly seems to have less memory and storage space on the hard drive.

o  Your default web page has been changed without you knowing it.

o  You notice a new toolbar in your browser and find it difficult to remove.

o  Disks or drives are inaccessible.

o  Your computer starts to freeze or crash at unexpected times.

o  You have difficulty printing items correctly.

o  Your antivirus program cannot run on your computer or cannot be installed.

It is very important to note some legitimate software can cause these problems as well, so the only real way to know if your computer is virus-free is to run an anti-virus program and scan all of your files. If you find your computer is infected with some kind of malicious software, remove it as soon as possible. This can sometimes be accomplished by simply running your anti-virus or anti-spyware programs. These programs will normally remove or quarantine the infected files and programs and clean your system of the threat. In some cases though, your computer may need a "professional cleaning" of sorts. This is when the infected files cannot be removed by normal anti-virus programs and will need a computer professional to resolve the problem. In severe cases, a complete wiping (erasing) of your hard drive may be necessary to completely remove the threat.

It is highly recommended to back up your files periodically in the event that something should happen to your computer. An external hard drive can be purchased at most stores for a relatively small cost and can provide an easy back up for if/when your computer becomes infected.

# CHAPTER 8:

# MOBILE DEVICE SECURITY

These days it seems like everyone has a smartphone or tablet or some other mobile device that can access the Internet. The ability to have access to the world wide web in the palm of your hand is incredibly useful and convenient. You can easily search for directions if you need to find your way or order take-out while already on the road. Mobile devices such as these help connect people with the world or do their jobs outside of the office every day.

This ability to connect from anywhere also brings the concern about how to keep these devices secure and your data safe. This chapter is more about protecting the phone if it should be lost or stolen as opposed to a virus or spyware, but we'll discuss both.

The evolution of mobile devices shows no signs of slowing, and with each new generation, the devices become more efficient tools that people increasingly rely on to conduct both their corporate and personal business. Apps that allow the user to access sensitive corporate data are prime targets for hackers and provide a wide range of access ports to data. Controlling security breaches of mobile devices is complex due to the varying software and device types. Additionally, many organizations have no restrictions on use of personal devices.

## Why do I need to worry about my phone's security?

Imagine that your smartphone is lost, or your tablet is stolen. Other than the money spent on purchasing the device itself, what else is thrown out the window?  That depends on the amount of sensitive personal data you have stored on there.

Do you have your email account linked to it? Your social networking site? Bank account log-ins? You get the point. The real issue isn't necessarily how much information you have on there.  Instead, you should be asking yourself, what protections do you have in place to prevent unauthorized access to your information?

> ### Did you know?
> More than 1 in 3 users of mobile devices worldwide has had a device lost or stolen.

On average, people claim that the data stored on their mobile devices is worth about $37,000.  This data includes music files, photos, account data, contact information, email addresses, and more. What value do you place on your device? Wouldn't you want to protect something so valuable?

Not only is there personal information on there, but if you use your phone for work related activities, then you potentially have critical information related to your business.  Cyber-thieves will be eager to steal this information and use it for themselves. Just like hackers who continually target large corporate networks in hopes of compromising their computers and stealing personal information, the same happens with mobile devices. Actually, it is becoming more common for hackers to try to use a smartphone or tablet to access those networks due to the sometimes lacking security measures in place on corporate networks and devices.

Criminals are already creating tainted apps and it appears that the most exploited operating system (OS) for these apps in the Android platform. Security professionals have found that there are more holes and potential vulnerabilities in this OS than in any other so far. This explains why most of the potentially malicious apps are found in this market.

These criminals are finding ways to hack into a person's mobile device. Then, when that person logs into their corporate network, the criminal can gain access to a multitude of information and data. This is why many businesses are struggling to stay ahead of the technology and prevent attacks like this from happening.

Of particular concern on a personal level is location-tracking technology that is built into the latest smartphone and tablet models. Nearly one-third of the web apps available make use of location data that can pinpoint the exact location of the user.

This readily available information has introduced unprecedented privacy and legal concerns. Criminals are finding ways to track users whereabouts and potentially find them in person. As the technology improves and new built-in features are developed, more and more unintended side effects come to light.

## Phones are computers, only smaller.

The first step to protecting the information on your mobile device is to realize that these devices are really computers, only smaller. They connect to the Internet, run applications and store data. Therefore, you need to have security settings in place just like you would for your PC.

Smartphones are slightly different, though, in that unlike computers where each application or executable file can access the information in other applications (viruses seeing everything on your computer), most mobile devices give apps their own work environment, meaning it is a stand-alone application and cannot access other apps' data. Because of this, malicious software can do very little harm to the other programs on your mobile device simply by being installed. This is a huge security upgrade over regular computers, but it is not foolproof.

This feature of not being able to access other apps' data is also one of the biggest problems with using a traditional anti-virus program. On a regular computer, these programs scan your entire computer system and all applications and programs. If it can't access the files of all of the apps on your mobile device, then its effectiveness is severely limited. There are antivirus programs available for these devices, though. These programs also offer more security features than just the antivirus protection.

A new program developed by Symantec will allow you to lock or wipe a phone that becomes missing simply by sending a coded text message. Another message causes the phone to respond with its location—a benefit of the location-tracking software—including a link to view the location in Google Maps. This program also has a SIM card lock feature which means that a thief can't change out the phone's SIM card without a password, rendering the phone useless to them. This particular program only works on the Android platform but Symantec does offer a similar version for the iOS for Apple products as well.

## Malicious software: there's an app for that.

To date, there have not been any real viruses on modern

smartphones. This could be a result of the Mac-effect, where there were simply not enough of the same brand of phone or operating system to make it worth trying to hack into. With the ever increasing number of smartphones and tablets on the market today though, this threat will be increasing and it will eventually happen.

With that said, mobile devices face a different type of threat. Over the past few years, apps have been developed which can read and transmit information from the phone to someone else. There have been cases where rogue apps have landed on devices and read your contacts and send them off to a third-party. These things are always evolving, so it is only a matter of time before something comes on the market that can do even more complex things. Just like Macs used to be immune to problems and are now prone to attacks, the same can be said about mobile devices.

Advertising agencies are getting in on the act too. Many companies have created apps that will bombard you with annoying alerts or obtrusive text advertisements. Some even change your ringtone to blurt out their advertising message when your phone rings. Some of these protection programs can now search your device for these apps and remove them or at least disable their ability to control your device.

## How do I secure my phone?

There are a number of things you can do to protect the security of your phone. Many of these are the same things listed in Chapter 5:

o Keep all software up to date, including the operating system and installed apps. This helps protect the device from attack and compromise.

o Enable access protection such as a PIN or password. This will lock your phone and prevent someone else from having access to it without knowing the codes.

o Set an idle timeout that will automatically lock the phone when not in use. This also helps prevent unauthorized individuals from gaining access to your data.

o Disable features not in use such as Bluetooth, infrared or WiFi. This will prevent you from automatically connecting to networks and will also save your device's battery life.

o Be wary of any files, links or messages sent from an unsolicited source.

o You may want to disable the mobile GPS location tracking on your phone. This allows certain programs to automatically know where you are at all times.

o Check the reputation of apps before downloading and installing them to be sure they are from trusted sources. Also review the privacy policies of the apps before downloading.

o Avoid using untrusted / unencrypted WiFi networks. This can cause programs and apps to be automatically installed on your computer without you knowing it.

o Do not "jailbreak" or "root" your device. "Jailbreaking" and "rooting" removes the manufacturer's protection against malware. It is best to not mess with the default security settings.

o Enroll your device in *"Find My iPhone"* or an equivalent service. This will help you locate your device should it be lost or stolen.

o If your device supports it, ensure that it encrypts its storage with hardware encryption. In conjunction with "Find My iPhone," this can allow data to be removed quickly in the event that the device is lost or stolen.

o Turn off the auto-fill and cookies on your device. This can be a privacy threat.

For the most part, mobile devices are secure and useful items if you take the precautions listed above. The most important thing you can do is keep the Operating System and apps up to date. If these programs become outdated, the vulnerabilities can be exposed and taken advantage of and your device could be compromised or hacked into.

When not using your mobile device, be sure to keep it in a secure location to prevent it from being lost or stolen.

## Be prepared in case of losing your device.

We all have the fear of losing our mobile devices and by taking a few precautions ahead of time, we can have a better chance of recovering the device if it were to ever be lost or stolen.

Here are several things you should do with your new device as soon as you get it home from the store.

o Write down the serial number or any other device specific identification numbers. These numbers cannot be changed on most devices and will help when reporting lost or stolen devices.

○ Take a few pictures of the device. This is so you have a visual record, which will help when identifying the device and in case insurance companies require it.

○ Write down the make and model of the device. It helps to know exactly what you had.

○ Keep a copy of the receipt and keep it with other important documents.

○ Register your device in either Apple's Find my iPhone application or Microsoft's Find a Lost Phone service. If this is not done BEFORE your device is stolen, it will be useless.

Doing these things will not prevent your mobile device from being stolen, but it will help you find it again if you ever do misplace it.

## What should I do if my phone is lost and/or hacked?

So, you were out at dinner and left your phone on the table when you left. By the time you got back, it was gone. That phone was everything to you, your telephone book, photo album, email program, banking center, MP3 player and more. Now it's gone. What do you do?

The answer to this really depends on what precautions you put in place before the phone was stolen. If you did nothing to your phone except get it out of the box and start using it, then the phone is most likely lost for good with very little chance of ever finding it again—unless you are fortunate enough to have someone turn it in and return it to you.

If you did register if with Apple or Microsoft or any other third-party program, you should be able to use their services to locate and lock down your device. Most of these programs allow the user to track the smartphone or tablet using the built-in GPS system—if turned on. They also let you lockdown the device from further use and send messages to the person who might have found/taken it.

Do not hesitate to call police and file a report. While the police may not be able to spend the time to track down every lost phone or tablet, if you have an official report of the theft, it will help you later.

Lastly, be sure to contact your mobile service provider. Let them know what happened so that they can lock down the phone for you, if you haven't already.

In 2012, all four major U.S. cellphone carriers agreed to deny cell and data service to stolen phones and to contribute the serial numbers of those phones to a national mobile device database. This will allow users to deny voice, data and SMS access to any individual phone or tablet, all while keeping your account intact and avoiding a full SIM block. This is added evidence of why you should take note of the serial number and identifying information on the phone and store it somewhere safe so that you can report that information to your carrier.

# PART III:

# PROFESSIONAL RISKS

So far, this book has discussed risks and threats pertaining to the here and now. All of the items discussed so far can have an impact immediately and generally happen right as you are working online. This segment of the book references things you may or may not think about when working online or playing on your social networking site. These are the risks with the potential to affect your future, whether it is a few days from now, several months down the road or even many years in the future. They are meant to make you think about what you do today and how it could affect what happens tomorrow.

# CHAPTER 9:

# COLLEGE ADMISSIONS, JOB HUNTING AND ONLINE REPUTATION

One of the most exciting times in a young person's life is when they are trying to get into a college or land their first job. The stresses of scoring highly on tests and focusing on getting good grades or even tweaking your resume to be just right is more than enough for anyone to pull their hair out. But, there is information about you which can have just as much of an impact, if not more, than your academics and work experience.

Whenever you meet someone new and want to find out more about them, what's the first thing you do? If you are like most people, you'll jump on the Internet and do a search for their name. You then browse through the different items listed in the search results and form an opinion about them. Whether or not you are correct in your assessment of the individual, your first impression was formed by the information found on the Internet. You can assume then, when someone wants to learn something about you, they would do the same thing. Your online reputation, therefore, plays an important role in personal and professional life and has become a significant factor in recruitment decision making.

# Why is this something you should be concerned about?

The majority of the teen and young adult population ages 13 – 22 have a profile on a social networking site. Many of you probably have more than one profile on more than one site. Your profile most likely contains funny quotes made by you or someone you know, pictures from your social life, postings from friends and family, etc. This information is all fun and exciting when sharing it with your other friends and people you socialize with. But are they the only people looking at this information? Have you ever considered how this information might be viewed from an outside source? Have you ever considered the concept of representatives from the place you want to attend school or the business you just applied for a job at viewing this information? It is becoming more and more common for potential employers and college admissions officers to check online profiles of applicants to see what the individuals are like on a more personal level.

These profiles and other online information about you are often times the first interaction these officials will have with you. And don't think they won't look. They will. Will it be a good first impression? As the saying goes, "you never have a second chance to make a first impression."

## College Admissions:

Nearly 25 percent of admissions officers admitted to viewing profiles on social networking sites in order to evaluate applicants. That is one in four! If your profile is one of the ones being looked at, what impression will it leave?

About forty percent of the officers surveyed who viewed the profiles admitted what they saw negatively affected their views of the applicant. Only a quarter of the respondents said their views of the potential student were improved.

This goes to show that even if you have a 4.0 GPA and scored a perfect 1600 on your SAT, you could still be turned away because of something about you posted online. An admissions officer at a local college told me about something they encountered. This officer

### Did you know?

Nearly 25% of admissions officers admitted to viewing profiles of prospective applicants.

was looking online for some feedback on his school. A person who had submitted an application to the school submitted a review. The officer tracked down the student's social network profile and saw the student was overly confident and felt he had aced the application process. The student went on to say he really didn't want to attend the school even after the application was submitted. The admissions officer decided to reject the applicant based on this information.

This probably sounds like a foolish reason to turn someone away, but it does happen. Unfortunately, this is not an isolated incident either. Cases such as this happen all across the country and in all types of institutions. It is very difficult to judge the real personality of a person when you see them both in person and through their online persona. How do you know which is real and which is just a made up façade? It is even harder to determine a person's true personality if the only interaction is through online profiles. Things posted online cannot always be proven or disproven, so finding validity in certain statements can be difficult. With that in mind, do you really want to risk someone making a wrong (or in some cases accurate) impression of you based solely on what is on your profile?

Admissions offices across the country continually receive thousands of applications each year for entry into their school. Because of this high volume, they will not be looking at every individual applicant's online reputation. Most admissions officers will only search for more information on an applicant to learn more about a project in which they were involved, or because a red flag was raised in an interview, recommendation or somewhere else.

But who's to say they won't randomly select a few to browse. The type of school does not make a difference either. Ivy League schools, community colleges, public universities. Any one of them could easily take a few extra minutes to browse the Internet when deciding who to accept and who not to accept. Recent trends are showing that the more selective the school, the more likely your profile or online information will be viewed. Is it fair? Maybe. Acceptable? Depends. Legal? You bet.

Most schools do not have a policy regarding the browsing of applicant profiles, nor are they really in a hurry to develop them. This lack of direction leads to a variety of standpoints on whether or not this practice should be allowed, or even expected. Information posted on the Internet is considered public and available for anyone to view. Therefore, most admissions officers consider the information found on these networking sites to be public knowledge and have no issues with looking at it to help them in their decision making process. Others, though, are a little more old-school and are uncomfortable flipping through the pages of other people's profiles. Unless this practice becomes unacceptable or deemed to be illegal (unlikely to happen), you should assume someone other than your friends and family will, at some point, be viewing your profile to see what you are like. As was stated before, will they get a true impression of who you are?

Many colleges have created their own online presence in these social networking programs. Most of the large public universities throughout the country have profile pages and use them to promote the school and any activities going on. These pages are a great way for potential students to find out more about the school and to ask questions or join in on a public discussion. While these pages are typically public so anyone can view the content, it is not uncommon for people to still "friend" the school to show their support. If you are one of those people who are now "friends" with your school, you have now opened the door for them to view your profile. If you have nothing embarrassing on your page, then you have nothing to worry about. But, since you now know admissions officers are browsing prospective student's profiles, will what they see affect their decision?

In an effort to turn the tides a little bit, many users on social networking sites use pseudonyms instead of their real names.  This could be beneficial if you are trying to hide from people. However, even if you do this, remember that there are ways to track down users based on phone number or email address (both of which would be readily available on a college application). So even if you don't use your real name online, you can be found if someone really wanted to look for you.

### How can you change your profile to be more college admissions friendly?

While many admissions officers admit that what they find online reflects poorly on the applicant, some have noted that their impressions of the potential student actually improved based upon what they found.  While each person will be different in their assessment of what is helpful and what is detrimental to your reputation, here are a few things you can do to your profile to make it more inviting and professional and reduce the risk of being denied:

- o Make your profile rated PG.
- o Remove or block any photos showing you drinking alcohol, even if it was legal.
- o Remove or block any photos showing you intoxicated or containing rude gestures or sexually suggestive content.
- o Unsubscribe from any groups showing bias (the ones like "I hate John Doe" or "It's 5 o'clock somewhere").
- o Remove contact information such as phone number or home address. This is not only a safety issue listed in earlier chapters, but it also shows poor judgment on your part.
- o Choose a professional looking photograph to use as your profile picture. Sometimes, this is the only access they have to your profile and you want to make a good impression.
- o Un-tag yourself from any videos or photos with the ability to have someone form a bad impression of you.

While it is true you can block access to your account and prevent many of these people from viewing your profile, it never hurts to do some house cleaning and make your profile more "visitor friendly." An even better idea would be to take advantage of this resource and make your profile an extension of your application and promote yourself on it. Provide information about work you have done or show pictures of doing constructive things or trips you have taken. Social networking sites do not have to be harmful to your reputation. If used correctly, they can greatly benefit you in many professional ways.

## Job Hunting:

Just like with college admissions, job recruiters and Human Resource representatives are constantly browsing the Internet for information on potential new hires while trying to narrow down their candidate pool. This doesn't mean employers are looking up every single applicant. That would be unrealistic. Most companies will still complete their normal process of reviewing resumes and cover letters and base their initial selection on experience and education. The next step in the process used to be to call the candidate and invite them in for an interview or even conduct a phone interview with them. However, times have changed and step two in the process has evolved into conducting a quick Internet search for the final candidates before calling any for an interview.

Recruiters these days are looking for more than just a good GPA or evidence of your previous work experience. They are also looking for the intangibles—your personality, interpersonal and character skills, etc. These are things they cannot teach you, but instead are natural and make you the person you are. They also cannot be easily conveyed through the few paragraphs of a cover letter or in the detailed information of your resume. Job recruiters know your generation is tech savvy. They know they can teach you any kind of computer program needed. But, how do they teach you how to be tactful in conflict or have a decent sense of humor? It is this type of information they are hoping to find when they do these Internet searches and browse the social networking sites.

Don't believe us? Here is a first-hand experience I was involved in which proves this point. I used to work at a television station (before entering the computer / tech support industry) which received dozens of applicants for internships each semester. These applicants were primarily college sophomores or juniors who were looking to gain experience in the field. The station employees did the normal narrowing of the candidates based on the content of their letters and resumes. When we had our selection down to the top five or so candidates, we looked them up online to see what else we could find out about them. We wanted to be sure they would fit in with the people in the office and would not be a distraction. I remember distinctly one of the individuals I researched was a member of a fraternity and the school's band. So far, so good. However, on the next item I found his social networking page. His profile had the appropriate privacy settings selected so all I could see was his profile picture. That was all the information I needed. The picture showed him in a less than flattering pose in an obviously drunken state. They say a picture is worth a thousand words. This one definitely told me a pretty good story. Needless to say, this particular applicant did not get the position. The position was given to someone else whose information online was more professional and mature.

Was I correct in my judgment? I'll never know. Since he did not get the position, I never met him personally and did not get a chance to know what he was really like. It is possible the only picture I saw was the exception to the rule and it reflected the only crazy night out he had ever had. Unfortunately for him, I had no way of knowing anything more than what I saw and based my decision only on what I found. I am not alone in my research of candidates.

In a recent study, nearly 86% of all Human Resource professionals surveyed in the U.S. admitted to researching candidates online. In stark contrast, only 7% of Americans believed their online reputation and information found about them online affected their ability to obtain employment. More and more companies are developing formal policies actually encouraging or requiring the HR professionals to research candidates online. Even if the company does not have a

> ## Did you know?
>
> 86% of all Human Resource professionals admitted to researching candidates online.

formal policy, the recruiters will still, more often than not, search for reputational information about the applicant.

### What do these recruiters look for?

In this difficult job market you want to be able to maximize your chances of being selected for a position. Understanding what information is out there and how it can affect your employment chances is critical now more than ever. Companies are constantly concerned about their image and know their employees are an extension of their business and therefore play a great role in how the reputation of the company is conveyed. Because of this, the hiring process has evolved to include social behavior and reputation as well as job performance.

Listed below are some of the top reasons HR professionals rejected a candidate after researching them online. This is not a full list, but gives an understanding of the types of things recruiters look for in determining if a candidate is acceptable for a position with their company or not:

- o Concerns about the candidate's lifestyle.

- o Comments and text written by the candidate deemed inappropriate.

o Inappropriate photos and videos posted online.

o Inappropriate comments and text written by friends or family of the candidate.

o Affiliation with certain groups or organizations.

o Providing false information online.

o Misspelled words and poor grammar.


Something of some concern is the lengths recruiters and HR professionals will go to in order to find out information about potential candidates. They seem to be very comfortable searching for information which would be completely unethical and sometimes illegal to ask a candidate to provide. Things such as information about their families, affiliation to religious, political or other groups, any medical conditions, or even financial information are all considered fair game in these online searches. Since this information is found on the Internet, it is considered public information and therefore is not bound by many of the laws currently in place.

The amount of information you can find out about someone online is remarkable, if not down-right scary. Have you ever done an Internet search for yourself? What came up in the search results? Most likely you saw your social networking profile, a website (if you have one) and anything else you may have posted somewhere or were affiliated with (blogs, organizations, etc.). It is possible you find things you posted or did five or ten years ago, or longer. If you had such an easy time finding this information, you can bet it is the same for anyone else trying to locate information about you.

## What can you do to improve your Online Reputation?

There are many things you can do to prevent employers, or anyone else for that matter, from forming a false representation of your true self. There are differing views as to who should be responsible for a person's online reputation. Some people feel it is the user's responsibility and they should be held accountable for what they post online. Others, though, feel it is the responsibility of the websites themselves to protect the content and privacy of the consumers using their pages. In any event, here are a few examples of things you can do to turn potentially negative influencing information into positive reinforcement of your personality.

### Social networking sites:

One of the easiest ways to protect your image is to separate your personal and professional lives. If you have a social networking profile for your friends to view, create a new one strictly for professional use. Set your privacy settings to the highest level for the personal one, but keep the professional page public so anyone can access it and see what a great person you are. On your professional page, you would want to highlight your skills and keep it formal and mature. Join groups or clubs reflecting a positive attitude. It also helps to have a more professional looking layout and color scheme for your profile. Keep in mind, though, this page is public, so be sure to limit the amount of personal information you provide.

### Remove old websites:

If you ever created a website containing information you

did not want to be shared, remove the site if at all possible. This can be easier said than done, though. As with all things on the Internet, once something goes online, it stays online. Even if you only posted something for a day and then removed it, the page or content is still available to the rest of the world because of something called caching. Caching is basically storing information which was put on the Internet and keeping it. Do an Internet search for any topic you want. Beside each of the search results will be a link called "cached" or something similar. This is a version of that particular website at a specific date and time. This cached version is always available on the Internet, even if the page you are looking for is no longer active. Website caches are often updated, so it is logical to believe the page you want removed will eventually disappear, but there is no way of knowing if or when that will happen.

It is possible to have this information removed manually, but there is sometimes a lengthy process involved when dealing with the search engine companies. And, just because you have the item deleted from one search engine, doesn't mean it won't show up in another. Having your information always available is the risk of putting anything online today. It is nearly impossible to completely remove.

**Change or remove content:**

Another way to clean up your online reputation is to simply change the wording of some of the writings you may have posted somewhere. Changing the text and wording can usually help in lessening the impression of what someone reads. This could be a daunting task if you continually reply to discussion boards or operate a blog of some sort. Removing embarrassing videos of yourself from a video sharing website is a step in the right direction too.

Regardless of whether it is an accepted practice or not, the concept of people making impressions about you—for better or worse—based upon what they find on the Internet should concern you. This is not suggesting you completely do away with your profile on your social networking site or you stop using blogs or posting videos or doing whatever else you do online. On the contrary, these social networking sites and blogs can be very beneficial and you should use them to their highest potential.

However, you should think about what you are putting online. The next time you post something online, think about these questions before sending it off into cyberspace for eternity:

- Why are you doing this (sharing information online)?
- Is now the best time to be doing this?
- Where do you draw the line between private and public?
- Do you really want a stranger seeing this?
- Do you want to be a part of a controversy?
- Do you really want this information available in 5, 10, 20 years?

If you can justify the reasoning, then by all means, put whatever you want online. Just remember, as the studies show, online reputation is increasingly becoming a factor in job recruiting and college admissions decision making for either accepting or rejecting a candidate. While these might not be risks affecting your physical well-being, they have just as much of an impact—if not more—on your social and professional goals as any of the other risks outlined in this book.

# CHAPTER 10:

# COPYRIGHT AND PLAGIARISM

If you have ever written a research paper for school, you have probably heard lectures about copyright and plagiarism or have at least heard the terms before. You were most likely warned not to copy someone else's work or else you would fail the paper or have more severe consequences. But were you ever really told what Copyright and Plagiarism really are? You were told the basics: if you use someone else's work you must cite it correctly or else it is being used illegally. In general terms, this is true. But these laws do not just play a role in writing. Any kind of media, be it print, radio or video, is usually protected by copyright law. The word "usually" is used because, like any rule, there are exceptions, which are discussed a little later.

## Why should you care about copyright laws?

If you ever write a paper or download music or movies or share files of any kind, you need to be aware of what copyright is and how it can affect you. You do not want to get caught by having illegal copies of a program or file. The law does not care if you knew it was illegal or not. In their eyes, if it is a copyright infringement, it does not matter on the intent, only the fact that you did it. A judge isn't going to care if you were robbing a bank to feed your family. The fact you committed the crime would be enough to put you in jail. The same can be said about copyright and plagiarism. If you know the rules, you are less likely to find yourself in any serious trouble. It is a much bigger issue than most people are willing to admit.

## What is copyright?

By definition, copyright is "the exclusive legal right to reproduce, publish, sell, or distribute the matter and form of something (as a literary, musical or artistic work)." Basically, this means only the person who creates or writes the original document or artistic work has the authority to reproduce it, distribute it, or display it publically in any form. The research paper you just turned in? It is protected by copyright. No one else can use the exact same paper, or portions of it, without your permission. If they do use it and claim it as their own, they have committed plagiarism, which is a whole separate topic which is discussed in more detail later on in the chapter. But first, it is important to understand more about what copyright is.

Before this discussion gets too much farther, it is important to add a little disclaimer about the content of this chapter. The information in this chapter is accurate and true to the best of the author's knowledge. However, this information should not be used to make legal decisions of any kind. For a full review of the copyright laws, please refer to the United States Government website for copyright, www.copyright.gov. All right, with the disclaimer taken care of, it is time to move on to the nuts and bolts of copyright.

Copyright laws were formed in the United States as far back as 1790 when our founding fathers wrote the US

Constitution. Article I, Section 8 of the Constitution states "Congress shall have the power... To promote the Progress of Science and useful Arts, by securing for limited Times to Authors and Inventors the exclusive Right to their respective Writings and Discoveries." This means the original creator of a work is given the exclusive right to do what they please with it, but no one else can have that same right for that particular piece of work.

Originally, this was meant to cover only literary works as the technologies for audio and video recordings did not exist at the time. However, over the years, Congress has passed new Copyright protection laws to include other types of works which have emerged with new technologies. Not sure what can be copyrighted? Anything fitting into one of the following eight categories is protected by copyright laws:

1. Literary works – not limited to only literature.
2. Pantomimes and Choreographic works.
3. Pictures, graphics, sculptures.
4. Sound recordings.
5. Motion pictures and video productions.
6. Computer programs.
7. Compilations of works.
8. Architectural works.

Along with things able to be copyrighted, there are several things which do not fall into those categories and are therefore not protected by copyright laws. Section 102 of Title 17 of the US Copyright law states "in no case does copyright protection for an original work of authorship extend to any idea, procedure, process, system, method of operation, concept, principle, or discovery, regardless of the form in which it is described, explained, illustrated or embodied in such work." This means your favorite cake recipe cannot be copyrighted. Nor can your procedure for tying your shoes be copyrighted. Things such as a phone book can also not be considered copyrighted material because the book is comprised of information considered to be facts and are therefore public knowledge.

## Is a work protected by copyright laws forever?

No. All copyrights have an expiration date of some sort. For most works created after 1978, that date is 70 years from the date the author or artist dies. So, if your favorite author has a book you want to copy and he dies in 10 years, the book is still protected by copyright for 70 more years after his death. If the work was created by a corporation or by an incorporated individual, their copyright is now either 95 years from the date of publishing or 120 years from the creation date, whichever is shorter.

Any item created before 1978 will fall under slightly different copyright laws. As mentioned, these laws have changed over time and with each change came a change in the lifespan of the copyright itself. If you are not sure about whether a creative work is protected under copyright, find out the year the work was published or created and look up the copyright laws for that time. Once a copyright expires, the work enters into the Public Domain, which basically means it is able to be copied and used by anyone for any reason.

## What is the Public Domain?

The Public Domain is the collection of literary and other works which are no longer protected by copyright. Any item in the Public Domain can be freely used, distributed, copied, or performed without fear of any penalties. Work can become a part of the Public Domain in many different ways. For instance, as mentioned above, once the copyright for a work expires, it automatically enters the Public Domain. The original creator can also essentially donate their work to the Public Domain and allow people to use it without needing permission.

There are also several types of works which do not fall under any copyright protection at all and are put in the Public Domain from the start. These include works created by the Federal Government, any published works created before 1923 and any unpublished works created before 1883. These works are able to be copied and used without the need to gather permissions. This doesn't mean you do not need to cite them in your work though. Plagiarism laws are not the same as copyright.

## Fair Use

One exception to the copyright rule blurred the lines between what is allowed and what is not allowed when using someone else's works. It is the practice of Fair Use of copyrighted materials. It turns out there are situations where you can copy and use parts of someone else's work without their permission—notice it does not say the entire work. However, these situations can be up for interpretation by different individuals and what you see as Fair Use, might not be how someone else sees it.

In education, Fair Use is extremely useful while working on research papers, video projects and other school related activities. In many cases there are materials out there you might want to use to "liven up" your project. When you come across something you want to use, you'll need to determine if it will be considered Fair Use. To do this, consider the following factors.

1) **The purpose and character of the use**.

   a. Is the portion used for a non-profit educational purpose (Fair Use) or will it be used for commercial and money-making ventures (not Fair Use)?

2) **The nature of the copyrighted work.**

   a. Is it considered factual or creative? The less creative a work is, the more likely it will be considered to be Fair Use. Many courts consider this to be the least important of the Fair Use factors.

3) **The amount and substantiality of the portion used in relation to the copyrighted work as a whole.**

   a. How much of the original work was used? The more you copy, the less likely it will be considered Fair Use.

4) **The effect upon the potential market for or value of the copyrighted work.**

   a. Is the new work targeted towards the same audience as the original? Will you be taking business away from the original author by recreating the materials?

Each of these factors is separated from the others, yet they are all co-related. One factor by itself might go against the Fair Use argument for a particular work. However, when that same factor is combined with the other three factors, the overall usage of the copied material may fall under the Fair Use guidelines. For example, if the purpose of a particular work is for educational use, you might be able to get away with using more of the original work than if it was for commercial use.

Fair Use is typically reserved for education, journalism and research related instances. If you are making a copy for your own personal entertainment or to make money, you will typically not be able to use the Fair Use defense. Even if something falls under the Fair Use rules, you should still cite the source to avoid any plagiarism issues.

Because there is sometimes a blurred line between what is and is not protected by copyright laws online, it is important to go into a little more detail about some of the more common instances where copyright infringement is likely to occur.

## Getting Permissions

If you are going to be using someone else's work and you cannot justify using it via the Fair Use factors, your only option would be to then obtain permission from the original author / creator. This can sometimes be difficult because you need to track down their information. For most printed materials, be it online or in physical form, the creator holds the copyright. If the resource you are looking to copy is found on the Internet, there is typically some type of contact information on the page which allows you to get in touch with the page's creator or administrator. However, in many cases, instead of the creator holding the copyright, the publisher of the work is given those rights. In these cases, if you are in need of permission to use a particular written document, your best bet might be to contact the publisher directly or contact the Copyright Clearance Center in which most publishers are a member. This center usually handles permission requests on behalf of its members. Fines for copyright infringement can easily reach thousands of dollars for each piece of infringed material.

## Copyright and the Internet

Online content is protected by the same laws as offline printed materials. The Internet provides us with a plethora of information sources at the click of a mouse. These resources are used every day for research, business purposes, and entertainment. The first thing to remember when browsing information and content on the Internet is that everything you see online was created by someone else. Unless, of course, you are browsing your own personal website in which you created everything from scratch. Just because something is in the so-called "public domain" of the Internet, does not mean it can be freely used and distributed by anyone else. All content on a website is protected by the same copyright laws protecting offline works. Even if the site does not have the copyright symbol—"©"—it is protected. Laws enacted in the 1980's provide protection to any original work whether it has the copyright symbol or not.

On any given website there are a number of items protected by copyright, some of which are obvious and some of which you might not consider. The obvious items are the actual text and media files associated with the page. Media files can include any and all graphics, advertisements, charts, graphs, audio or video files, etc. The text includes any blog postings, articles and comments.

Then there are the not so obvious things which are protected. These include the actual source code of a webpage, the design of a page (look and feel), and even the links. The actual URL of a link is not protected itself because it is considered to be a fact, but the link is protected because it contains unique text and styling not found in other places.

## Copyright and Music

Music is one of the most copyright protected and regulated forms of media. New technologies have made it so easy to obtain copies of your favorite song—both legally and illegally—the music industry is up in arms about how to stop it. Musical works are protected by the same laws as written documents, however, they are normally in higher demand. With the use of portable MP3 players, CDs, computers, and other devices, music files are easily loaded and transferred from device to device.

There are a number of Internet sites in which you can legitimately download songs. Many artists will allow you to download their latest songs or some of their favorites without you paying a penny for it. Other sites will charge a flat fee for their songs. This is typically around one to two dollars a song depending on the vendor you are purchasing it from. These forms of obtaining the music are perfectly legal and will not land you in any trouble.

Online file-sharing programs (peer-to-peer), on the other hand, are known to allow people to upload or download music without paying a fee. No matter which you do—upload or download—it is considered copying the file, which is illegal. Many of these programs clearly warn you about downloading these songs or other copyrighted materials. By doing so, you are doing it illegally and could be subject to penalties. The warnings do little to deter people from downloading and uploading content to share with others. If caught, the fines for downloading illegal copies of a music file can be steep.

There are cases involving the Recording Industry Association of American (RIAA), a trade organization representing the recording industry, which show how expensive it can be to illegally download music. According to their website, the RIAA states, in cases of civil penalties, a person who illegally uploads or downloads a musical piece is subject to a minimum fine of $750 per song.

Case in point: a federal appeals court in Texas made a decision forcing a college student to pay the RIAA $27,750 for songs she had downloaded and shared while she was in high school. The penalty was for the minimum $750 per song for the 37 songs she had shared over the past several years. Her naivety towards her actions of downloading and sharing these files was not a valid excuse in the eyes of the law. This person's lawsuit is just one of thousands of cases brought forth by the RIAA. The majority of these cases are settled out of court for far less than the actual minimum penalty would be if it went to a trial, but still average in the thousands of dollars.

Those are just the civil penalties. If a criminal lawsuit is brought against you, the potential is there for you to be sent to jail for several years. If the file-sharing or illegal usage of these music files took place using college, university, or employer owned resources, you could also face disciplinary actions by the school you attend or place of employment as well. These sanctions could include taking a class on copyright issues or even expulsion if the evidence supports it. Many businesses will fire you over the illegal use of their equipment.

## Copyright and Videos

Just like music, videos are a staple of online entertainment. Most Hollywood studios and television networks have their own websites and display either clips or entire episodes of your favorite shows. You can then view their pages and watch the videos without fear of doing anything wrong. However, if you were to copy the videos from these websites, you would be committing a major copyright infraction. These websites have embedded their videos so they are very difficult to save to your computer, but the possibilities are always there. Some not-so-advanced sites might not have the technology to be able to secure their videos online, making them prone to being copied. Those files are then distributed using the same file-sharing programs used to download and share music files. This illegal downloading or uploading of videos has the same potential penalties as you would have with the audio files.

To counteract this illegal downloading of videos, there are a number of websites which allow you to upload and view videos online and then even link your website to the file, providing better security for it. These websites work very hard to protect the integrity of their business by diligently searching for copyrighted materials and non-original works. Websites such as YouTube clearly mark in their Terms document the allowable usage of the videos found on their site. In Section 6, Item D, of their Terms it states "you further agree that you will not submit material that is copyrighted, protected by trade secret or otherwise subject to third party proprietary rights... unless you are the owner of such rights or have permission from their owner to post the material..." In many cases, the uploading of copyrighted material will simply lead to your account being terminated. However, if the owner of the copyright so chooses, they can pursue legal actions against you.

Those Terms cover you only while you are on their website though. What about when you see a video online and you want to provide a link to it or embed the video into your own personal website? Well, if you created the video and it contains all original material, then you can do as you wish with it. However, assuming you did not create 99.9% of the videos you see online, someone else will hold the copyright for the video you are viewing. For many of these videos, the person who originally uploaded the video can elect to either allow or not allow others to embed their video on other websites. It can be assumed—though perhaps wrongfully—if the owner allows the video to be embedded, they are willingly allowing it. In truth though, it is possible the owner simply overlooked that part of their uploading process and neglected to disengage the embed option.

If the video was posted by a major film studio or television network, it is in your best interest to not embed the video, even if the option is available. Instead, provide a link to the video and inform your visitors of what the link is for and why you are not embedding the video. While it is unlikely the networks have the time to browse every website out there for their videos, a lot of high-end websites have tracking software showing the website from which a file was accessed, including embedded videos. This makes it much easier to track down the sites containing their videos.

There is no hard and true answer to whether or not you can use someone else's video on your website. As with most types of content you find online, you need to be careful what you do with it. If you do not absolutely need to have the video on your site, then don't put it there. If you didn't create it and cannot get permission, you certainly should not use it.

## Internet and Web Pages

In this day and age, everyone seems to have their own

website. A quick Internet search will bring up a multitude of free website publishing programs. Even for the services which aren't completely free, there is usually very little cost involved in operating a website. With this in mind, websites on any type of subject are continually popping up on the web. If you ever looked closely at some websites, you will notice they look similar in design. In some ways this is inevitable because the most common layout for a website is the basic "box" look and there are only so many ways you can accomplish this design.

The general concept or idea of the layout is not necessarily protected by copyright. However, the design of a specific page is. What you see on your computer screen is the face of the website. As mentioned a few pages ago, everything you see on a website is protected by copyright. The only thing not protected is the actual URL of a link.

The specific layout of the page you are looking at is protected. Someone created the design using the layout, colors, fonts, or text-sizes displayed. While each of those things by themselves cannot be protected, the work as a whole is. You cannot copyright a color, or a font, or a text-size. Any images and graphics being used are also protected in two ways. The image placement is protected by the overall design of the page. The image itself is protected by the person who created it. The same can be said for any audio or video files and documents made available on the site. The files themselves are protected by the person who created them. Their placement is protected with the design of the page. You can only assume the publisher of the website was granted permission to use those files on their page and is not at risk of committing copyright violations for their content.

Along with the visual aspects of a website, the "guts" of a website are protected by copyright too. Just like snowflakes, there are no two web pages exactly alike. The only possible exception being scams—refer back to Chapter 6—but even those pages are different in many subtle ways. Each webpage has its own unique coding which molds it into the creation it is—its DNA, so to speak. What you see on the screen is a page full of text and graphics and photographs. But what really makes the website work is the source code. For those of you who are technically savvy, you know what the source code is and how to find it. For those of you who aren't, well, this book will not explain how to find it, but it will tell you what the coding shows you.

The source code tells you exactly how the webpage is made. It essentially is the blueprint for the design and all aspects of the page. It shows where all of the images are found and the different colors being used as well as other vital information. This code is what will be different from every other page. Believe it or not, this code is also protected by copyright laws. Someone created this page to look and work the way it does, making it unique. Their hard work is rewarded by not allowing someone to come along and copy their work.

As you can see, just about everything you hear, read or watch is protected by copyright. These laws are around to protect our individual creative rights and promote others to think for themselves instead of taking the ideas of others. While copyright protects the actual work from being copied and redistributed, plagiarism protects creative works from being copied and claimed as someone else's original work.

## Plagiarism

In layman's terms, plagiarism is taking someone else's work and claiming it as your own. This can include text from an article or book, ideas someone may have, songs a person may have written, story concepts for a movie or play, etc. Anytime you take from an original source without giving proper credit you commit plagiarism. This is an increasingly common and unfortunate occurrence when it comes to students and the Internet. Many people do not understand what plagiarism is or how to avoid it.

Here are some examples of ways you could commit plagiarism:

o Turning in a paper written by someone else and claiming it as your own.
o Using someone else's ideas without giving them credit.
o Not putting a quote in quotation marks.
o Providing incorrect information about the quote's source.
o Using the same sentence structure, but changing the words and not giving credit.
o Comprising the majority of your work from a single source, even if you gave proper credit.

A lot of times, people commit plagiarism and do not even realize what they did. Have you ever copied and pasted something from the Internet, changed a few words, and continued on with your work without citing where the information came from? You just committed plagiarism. Since the information did not come from your own mind and knowledge and you did not cite the source, you have committed plagiarism. If you give credit to your source, you are on the right path to not committing plagiarism. However, just citing something does not automatically get you off the hook. Unless you are using a quotation—in which case it better have quotation marks—all words you use in your paper or project should come from you. If they don't, it will most likely be considered plagiarism.

All of the copyright laws still apply when talking about plagiarism. When using other people's ideas or words, it is the same as when you are copying from something already created and is important to remember the Fair Use rules of the copyright laws. You'll need to consider the purpose and character of the use, the nature of the copyrighted work, the amount of the work you are copying / using, and the effect on the market of the copyrighted work.

This doesn't mean you need to cite the source of every fact and figure you put into your project. Things considered to be common knowledge do not need to be cited.

Penalties for plagiarism can be severe. If you are caught plagiarizing someone for a school project, you can easily be expelled for academic integrity issues. If you commit plagiarism while in a business setting, you would most likely lose your job. On top of being expelled or losing your job, you could also face thousands of dollars in fines and potentially jail time.

## People your age don't get caught with copyright infringements.

This could not be farther from the truth. In fact, people your age are looked at more closely to be sure you are not using someone else's work illegally. There are a number of stories about students being charged with copyright infractions and plagiarism.

Not long ago, an 18-year old University of Arizona student was sentenced to three months in prison, three months of probation, and was forced to serve over 200 hours of community service. Why? Because he had illegally obtained copies of copyrighted movies and music. This is not an isolated incident either. Situations like this happen all over the country.

One of the most common occurrences of copyright occurs in academia where students copy someone else's term paper or even obtain a copy of an upcoming exam. Anytime you use someone else's materials or obtain the copies illegally, you are committing copyright infringement and could be subject to some pretty severe penalties.

## How can you avoid copyright and plagiarism problems?

The best way to avoid getting in trouble for copyright or plagiarism laws is to simply write everything yourself and not use the ideas or words of other people. This is not always possible, especially when writing a research paper or other document where you need to rely on the information from other sources. In the situations where you are using information from another source, be sure to give credit where credit is due. Do not claim the work for yourself and do not copy it word for word. If your information came from a newspaper article, be sure to mention the exact article and newspaper. If the information came from a television program, be sure to cite that too. It is better to be safe than sorry when it comes to this type of activity. These laws are often times overlooked or completely forgotten about by many individuals who are writing documents or even sharing files on the Internet and can cost them dearly if caught.

# FINAL THOUGHTS

Everyone loves to play and work on the Internet. The games and social interaction it allows is second to none and provides us with a constant connection to the world. You are able to find out the latest on a breaking news story or read the most recent gossip about your favorite celebrity. More and more people are turning to the Internet to find that special someone and still more are on there simply to chat and make new friends.

The Internet is a very valuable resource and is vital to the world both socially and intellectually. This freedom of information and communication brings with it some dangers and risks you may not always think about. As was noted throughout the chapters of this book, there are a lot of things out there with the potential—and intent—to cause you harm. You now know more about what is out there and how you can protect both your personal well-being, as well as your property, from having anything bad happen. The best way to be safe online is to be proactive and vigilant about what you do. By being a little more careful about who you talk to and the information you provide online, you can ensure yourself of a safer journey while navigating the information superhighway.

Sure there might be a few fender-benders and speed bumps along the way, but with a little attention to detail, you can avoid the damaging collisions.

Safe Travels.

# ABOUT THE AUTHOR

Jeff Sechler has been working with computers and technology for over a decade. Most of his time is spent on the Internet and his experience and knowledge as an IT professional helps to provide guidance for many people. He spends much of his time advising peers and students about Internet safety best practices and how to keep their computers running smoothly. After several years of reiterating the same facts, he decided to provide them all in one easy-to-read book and share his knowledge with everyone else.